the
CHICKEN KEEPER'S
HANDBOOK

the
CHICKEN KEEPER'S
HANDBOOK

MARIA COSTANTINO

© 2011 Kerswell Farm Ltd

This edition published by King Books

Printed 2011

This book is distributed in the UK by
Parkham Books Ltd
27 The Oaklands
Tenbury Wells
Worcestershire
WR15 8FB

david@kingbooks.co.uk

ISBN: 978-1-906239-03-9

DS0192. The Chicken Keeper's Handbook

Creative Director: Sarah King
Project Editor: Sally MacEachern
Designer: Jade Sienkiewicz

Printed in Singapore

1 3 5 7 9 10 8 6 4 2

Contents

Introduction

As people have become more concerned and informed about the ways in which their food is produced, processed, preserved, packaged and presented to them on the shelves of supermarkets and
shops, many have made the decision either to buy certified organic, free-range and ethically produced
produce or to 'grow their own', and this includes keeping poultry for both their eggs and their meat.
Not only does this activity reduce the individual or family's carbon footprint, but it also makes for a
healthy way of life.

Chickens are probably the most widespread of all domestic animals, and today there are over two hundred different breeds, some developed specifically for egg production, some for their meat and others
purely for their beauty. They are popular because they are relatively inexpensive to feed and keep, and,
with a little forethought, you'll find that by selecting the right breeds for your particular circumstances
– your location or available space, for example – you can easily keep a few chickens or bantams in your
garden without causing any problems to your neighbours or your herbaceous borders. It's worth not-
ing, too, that these birds are pretty omnivorous and will happily eat up any household leftovers (except
for animal protein), and will feast on garden weeds, slugs and snails. All you need to provide is food,
water, a house and nest boxes, some shelter from the rain and sun and a dry dust-bath. In return, you'll
gain the freshest eggs, meat for your table and colourful additions to your garden and family.

This book will help to guide you through the processes of keeping chickens, from deciding on which
breeds to keep, through to choosing and buying your birds and then getting them home, to housing,
feeding and caring for them. It will also help you to decide on whether you want to breed and raise
chickens for their eggs or for the table.

CHAPTER ONE

The domestic chicken

Charles Darwin (1809–82), the author of the celebrated *On the Origin of Species by Means of Natural Selection* (1859), believed that the modern domestic chicken (*Gallus domesticus*) was descended solely from *Gallus gallus*, the red jungle fowl that is found over a large area, ranging from northern India and southern China into South East Asia. As a result of more recent DNA analysis, however, Darwin's 'one-bird-origin' theory has come into doubt because the gene that produces the yellow skin in domestic poultry does not come from the red jungle fowl, but more likely from *Gallus sonnerati*, the grey jungle fowl, which suggests that there was a possible cross between these two lines several thousand years ago.

Whatever the true origins of the domestic chicken, we know that it has been raised in captivity for some seven thousand years, archaeological excavations in northern China having uncovered bones dating to around 5000 BC, with excavations in north-eastern Thailand having revealed both red jungle fowl-type bones and bones from a Malay-type fowl dating to 3500 BC. Dating from around the same time, a wall painting from Egypt, from the tombs of Petosiris, depicts a cockerel being carried in a procession.

Chickens arrived in Europe in around 700 BC, and one of the earliest images of a chicken comes from a piece of decorated pottery from Corinth. The ancient Greeks believed that cockerels were so brave that even lions were afraid of them, and, in art, chickens became the attributes of Ares, the Greek god of war, as well as of the goddess Athena in her guise as the warrior-protector of the city-state of Athens. Chickens were reputedly introduced to Britain by the Romans between 55 BC and AD 43; we can assume that they were taken with Roman armies as provisions, but also for sport, cock-fighting being a widespread pastime.

The Romans also used chickens for many of their oracles: Cicero, writing in the first century AD, noted that it was a good omen if a chicken appeared, either flying or walking, from the left. The birds' feeding behaviour was also interpreted for its omens: the *pullarii* (the keepers of the sacred chickens) who tended to the birds gave them special food for this purpose, and if the birds ate it straightaway, the omens were favourable, but if they flapped about and refused to eat, then the omens were bad.

Lucius Junius Moderatus, a native of Gades in Spain, who is better known as the writer Columella, was the author of a treatise on agriculture dating from AD 65, in which he described keeping and breeding chickens. His recommendation was that flocks should consist of no more than two hundred birds (no doubt he envisaged them belonging to a large landowner, with many slaves), and that their coops

The arrival of chickens in Europe

should be adjacent to the kitchen, where the smoke from the fires would 'benefit their health'.

During the following centuries in the West, chickens were kept as farmyard fowl. These birds, which were reared for their eggs and meat, were the descendants of the birds introduced by the Romans, and also by the Vikings. As chicken-keeping was largely a small-scale and a domestic affair, there was no transfer of birds from one area to another for a long time, 'local' birds consequently interbreeding. And so it was that distinct breeds, such as the Dorking (from Surrey, England), the Crevecoeur (from the small town of the same name in Normandy, France) and the Drenth (from the Dutch province of Drenthe), emerged in different regions.

While remains of chickens found in Chile, in South America, that may date back to AD 1300 suggest the possibility that the Polynesians first introduced them to the New World, we know that Christopher Columbus took chickens with him on his second voyage there in 1493. And in 1607, early American colonists imported them to Jamestown, in Virginia, to provide eggs and sport (Americans did not consider the meat worthwhile eating until some time later).

During the mid-nineteenth century, European colonial expansion prompted the introduction to Europe of exotic 'oriental' breeds, such as the Cochin (with its novel brown eggs), from China, the Malay (from Asia) and the Brahma (originally from India, but brought to Europe from North America). At first, such exotic creatures were the preserve of wealthy landowners, their rarity and colourful plumage making them immensely valuable. Owning such birds – and breeding from them – meant that the owners had to secure certain features within their stocks so that one 'specimen' could be compared, and valued, against another.

The nineteenth-century passion for poultry reached fever pitch after Queen Victoria was given a pair of Cochins and began to keep a royal poultry yard. In 1846, the royal chickens were displayed at the Royal Dublin Agricultural Society's show, and the consequent press coverage made chicken-keeping extremely fashionable. An interest in describing and breeding the 'ideal specimen' soon arose, and, with it, the first dedicated exhibitions, shows and breeding clubs, the growth of which was further encouraged when cock-fighting was banned in Britain in 1849. In that year, too, the first North American poultry exhibition was held in Boston, attracting more than ten thousand visitors. The American Poultry Association was formed in 1873, and the following year the American standard of excellence was adopted.

Most of the time, chickens were still roaming freely around farmsteads, with their eggs being gathered by families and farmers for their individual needs, and any superfluous chickens being added to the pot. It was not until the end of the nineteenth century that the economic value of poultry began to be exploited, but even so, chickens were still generally being kept in flocks of no more than two hundred (Columella's ideal size), as well as being housed in hencoops at night, but being left to wander at will during the day, while all of the work of feeding and egg-gathering was done by hand.

The appliance of science

The scientific advances of the age had an equal impact on industry and agriculture during the nineteenth and twentieth centuries: improved henhouses and nutrition meant that although more eggs were being laid, the 'old-fashioned' breeds were not commercially viable because their eggs were small. So breeders looked now to the Mediterranean breeds that laid bigger eggs, with the introduction of the Leghorn from Italy vastly contributing to the development of poultry-farming.

With their demand for meat and eggs – and especially for eggs produced during the winter months – the new and growing urban markets prompted crossbreeding with imported Asiatic breeds, and from these, in turn, developed new breeds 'designed' for their utility (utility breeds lay plenty of eggs and grow to a decent size as table birds), such as the New Hampshire, the North Holland Blue, the Welsummer and the Barnevelder. These utility breeds are the 'traditional breeds' that once scratched around farmyards and smallholdings, and whose images graced many a picture book, but which were themselves superseded during the twentieth century by the modern hybrid chicken (although they were fortunately saved from extinction by hobbyist poultry-keepers).

The arrival of the modern hybrid hen signalled the end of the small henhouse and ushered in the era of the battery-hen and deep-litter systems of commercial 'free-range' poultry farms. These hens will lay an egg nearly every day for about two years, and will then stop laying; the factory farms will gen-

the chicken keeper's handbook

erally slaughter them at around eighteen months of age and will then bring in new birds because they don't want the expense of feeding the older birds during their annual moult, when they don't lay at all. The slaughtered birds are generally shredded and processed into foods – soups, for example – because there's not much flesh on them. It may sound heartless and cruel, but the harsh realities of feeding growing populations – particularly in the years following World War II – and the demand by consumers for inexpensive food have played their part in creating and sustaining this type of egg production.

Many people who are concerned about issues relating to animal welfare, food standards and sustainability in food production and in the environment are now growing – and raising – their own produce, including eggs and poultry meat. Keep chickens, and you won't make money from it, or even produce eggs or a roast chicken on the cheap. Your table birds will take six months before they are 'oven ready', not the six weeks (and the growth-hormone injections) required by factory-raised birds. You may not even be able to sell your surplus eggs or meat because there are strict laws against this in many countries (which change constantly), and besides, you'd have to inform the taxman. You could, however, trade some eggs for firewood or vegetables, but if you're sensible, you'll have just the right number of birds to satisfy your needs, with few, if any, being surplus to requirements.

CHAPTER

chicken basics

Now that you have decided to keep chickens, it's important to become familiar with the basics of chicken anatomy. Knowing the basics not only helps when you compare birds of the same breed, but it's vital to know exactly what a normal, healthy-looking chicken looks like so that you can spot any health problems or signs of disease before they spread to the rest of your flock.

Although the different breeds of poultry vary widely in their appearance, colouring and feather formation, they all share the same basic elements of anatomy: the 'points of a fowl', as shown on the picture opposite.

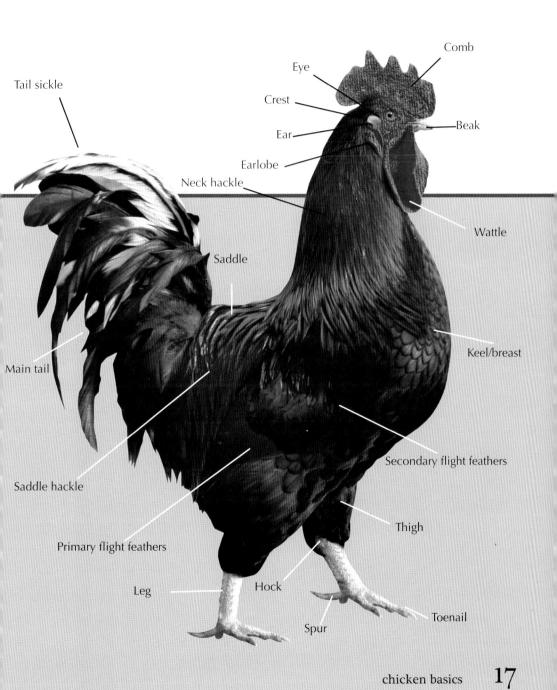

Tail sickle

Crest

Eye

Comb

Ear

Beak

Earlobe

Neck hackle

Wattle

Saddle

Main tail

Keel/breast

Saddle hackle

Secondary flight feathers

Primary flight feathers

Thigh

Leg

Hock

Spur

Toenail

the chicken keeper's handbook

Chickens and flight

Chickens are not keen flyers! Chickens are, of course, birds, and, with a few exceptions (penguins, kiwis and ostriches, for instance), birds can fly, including chickens, although most of the time they get around by walking. In fact, only a few chicken breeds will actually fly because the domestication process has made them placid, tame and ready to hang around humans on the off chance that some tasty morsel is offered. Furthermore, because breeding programmes have encouraged the production of birds with large bodies, their wings are not strong enough to raise and sustain them in extended flight, while those chickens that do get off the ground, like jumbo jets, need quite a long 'runway' before they can become airborne. Unlike jumbo jets that stay airborne, however, a chicken's weak wings will flap around for a minute or so before the bird drops back down to the ground. Do note, though, that there are always exceptions to the rule: there's always one chicken that manages to escape and has to be recovered some distance from home.

Even wild jungle fowl only fly when they have to, preferring to root around on the ground for food, but the presence of predators on the ground requires them to have safe, high-up roosting places for the night. Similarly, although most modern domestic chickens don't (or won't) fly, they, too, instinctively seek a high-up perch for the night.

Skeleton and skull

Like most birds, chickens have light skeletons made up of hollow bones that are designed to be light-weight for flight. Chickens have fourteen neck vertebrae that are highly flexible, allowing them to turn their heads through 180 degrees, as well as to move horizontally and vertically. But the bone that determines a chicken's overall shape is its breastbone: the length of the bone, and the degree to which the muscles on either side are developed, means that some birds will be broad-chested, while others will be more slender-fronted and delicate-looking.

The shape of a chicken's skull also varies from breed to breed. Game fowl generally have a short, broad skull; crested fowl, such as the Houdan and the fabulous Dutch Crested Fowl Bantam (which looks as though it's wearing a cheerleader's pompom on its head), have a lump of bone on the crown of their skulls called the crest knob, so there's more room for feathers on their heads.

Legs, feet and spurs

If you look at a chicken's legs, you'll see a hinged joint at the point where the feather-covered thigh meets the clean-skinned shank. This joint is called the hock, and it's the equivalent of the human ankle. (The actual knee in a chicken is higher up, at the top of the thighbone.)

At the bottom of the shank are the toes: in most chicken breeds, there are four toes, three of which are well spaced out and point forwards, with the fourth toe facing backwards to offer support to the body. Some breeds, however – like the Dorking, Faverolle, Silkie and Houdan – have an extra, fifth, toe. (This extra toe doesn't actually function because it's in a pretty useless place, located on the inside of the shank, above the fourth toe and pointing upwards.) Some breeds have their shanks and feet covered in feathers to greater or lesser degrees: Maranses have just a few feathers on their legs and feet, while breeds like the Dutch Booted Bantam are profusely covered and have long, stiff feathers at their heels called vulture hocks.

TOP: CHICKEN SKULL SHAPE VARIES FROM BREED TO BREED.
BOTTOM: THE JOINT AT THE POINT THE FEATHERED THIGH MEETS THE CLEAN-
SKINNED SHANK IS CALLED THE HOCK — EQUIVALENT TO THE HUMAN ANKLE.

THE CONES OF HORN, CALLED SPURS, ARE USUALLY FOUND ON COCK BIRDS.

Higher up the shanks (mainly in cock birds, but they do sometimes appear on hens) can be found the spurs. These are pointed cones of horn on the insides of the shanks that are used by cocks in fights to determine their order or rank in the flock. Spurs are usually blunt at the end, so no deep flesh wounds are inflicted, but in the days when cock-fighting was a sport, they were sharpened to lethal points or had metal blades attached to them. As the cocks grow older, their spurs grow longer, and they can interfere with the bird's freedom of movement. The spurs can be clipped away quite easily (and painlessly for the bird) with nail scissors because a spur consists of dead tissue (think of it as a long toenail), and only contains living tissue in the core, at the junction of the spur and the shank. In the same way as you wouldn't cut your toenails too short, the spur should be clipped short, but the live core should not be cut into.

Skin and leg colour

Most of us are familiar with the pale, white-skinned chickens that we see in butchers' shops and supermarkets. This colour is the result of breeding table birds to suit consumers' notions about what looks fresh, healthy and tasty. Yet there are plenty of skin-colour variations among chicken breeds: white-skinned breeds include Faverolles and North Holland Blues, and there are some breeds whose skin ranges from being very dark to almost black, such as the Silkie and the Ardenner. There are also yellow-skinned breeds, such as the Cochin, but don't confuse these yellow-skinned birds with dressed table birds that have been 'corn fed' to induce a yellow pigmentation. Truly yellow-skinned birds have the pigment in their epidermis, and this is also apparent in the yellow colour of their shanks.

Head furnishings: wattles, earlobes and combs

On a chicken's head is a variety of 'head furnishings': under the beak are the wattles, which, depending on the breed, can be long or short; in some breeds, a fold of skin called the dewlap can be found between the wattles; and at the side of the head are earlobes, which protect the chicken's ear ducts. A chicken's earlobes can be red, white or bluish in colour, and vary in size according to the breed. Surprisingly, it's earlobe colour that determines the colour of eggshells: a hen with white earlobes will generally lay white-shelled eggs, while a red-earlobed hen usually lays brown-shelled eggs. As always, there are exceptions to the rule, however: the Araucana, for instance, has red earlobes, but lays blue- or green-shelled eggs.

A FINE EXAMPLE OF A SINGLE COMB
IN THIS NORWECK COCKEREL

THE ROSE COMB OF A GOLDEN LACED WYANDOTTE

These areas of skin on chicken's heads are useful indicators of a bird's health. A bird that's in peak condition will have skin saturated with oxygenated blood, so that the colour and condition of the wattles, earlobes and comb will be bright and firm. But if a chicken's head furnishings are pale, this is a sign that the blood isn't circulating within the skin of the head, and that the bird is run-down and needs attention.

The most distinctive head feature of a chicken is the comb on top. Along with the wattles, the comb acts as a cooling system: birds can't sweat, so the chicken cools itself down by circulating 'hot' blood through its head furnishings, where it is cooled. There are several types or shapes of combs, as follows.

SINGLE COMB

The single comb is found in breeds like the Leghorn. The term describes a comb that stands upright on the head and has a number of serrations. The points of the comb are called spikes. Depending on the breed (and especially in laying hens), the single comb can be quite large, and the back part of it can droop to one side.

ROSE COMB

The rose comb is a low, broad comb without points that tapers off at the back into a single spike (in some countries, this spike is also called the leader), which can be seen gracing the heads of Wyandottes and Rhinelanders. Depending on the breed, the spike may follow the neckline or point straight back-

THE THREE-RIDGED COMB OF A BRAHMA

wards. It's also possible to have quite a fancy or accentuated rose comb, as does the Derbyshire Red-cap (whose name is a bit of a giveaway!)

'V'-SHAPED OR HORN COMB

The 'V'-shaped or horn comb consists of two vertical or backward-pointing 'horns'. The Brabanter Bantam and the ancient French breeds of chickens called Crevecoeur and La Fleche all have horn combs (the La Fleche is also nicknamed 'devil's head' on account of its 'satanic' horns!)

WALNUT OR CUSHION COMB

The walnut (or cushion) comb is a very descriptive name, for this comb does indeed look like half a walnut (there's no leader or spike) placed on the front of the chicken's head. The Twenthe Fowl and the Twenthe Bantam both have this type of comb.

PEA COMB OR THREE-RIDGED COMB

Related to the single comb, in its purest form, the pea or three-ridged comb comprises a single base with three low, lengthwise-running ridges (the middle one being a bit higher than the other two) and pea-like points. This type of comb can be seen on the Brahma, one of the largest chicken breeds.

BUTTERCUP AND LEAF COMBS

The buttercup comb is a little like a cross between a single comb and a 'V'-shaped or horn comb: it's formed by two single combs that have grown together at the front and back, as on the head of the delightfully named Sicilian Buttercup. But if the comb is fused together only at the front, it's called a leaf comb, as sported by the Houdan.

Feathers, feather colours and marking patterns

A chicken's feathers give it its distinguishing colours and silhouette or shape. Poultry breeds are categorised as being hard-feathered or soft-feathered (hard-feathered birds were those originally bred for cock-fighting, and these have smooth, close-fitting feathers). Not all chickens have the same amount of feathering: some may have feathers all the way down their legs, while others may have 'naked' legs; some may have feather 'beards' and crests'; and other breeds may appear to be missing feathers, like the naked-neck chickens from Eastern Europe.

Depending on the chicken's sex and where they are located on the body, the feathers will vary in shape, size and texture. The primary feathers, or flight feathers, are broad and long to provide lift and thrust, while down feathers are short and fluffy to provide insulation, the amount of which varies from breed to breed (Cochins have masses of down feathers that make them look much better upholstered than they actually are). Tail feathers are long and firm in structure, and – again depending on breed – can be very short or fabulously long. Feathers on the breast, back and wings tend to be fairly short and well rounded and act a bit like roof tiles: they shed the rain and keep the insulating down feathers dry. Hackles and neck feathers are soft, long and narrow. Maintaining the condition of their feathers is of great importance to chickens, and they spend a great deal of their time preening. This involves them having dustbaths and applying oil to their feathers taken from a gland at the base of the tail.

Providing as they do insulation and waterproofing, chicken feathers grow in many different colours and patterns. Just like the scales on a fish, the feathers – which are made of keratin, like hair and horns – overlap. The different colours and patterns of feathers help to identify and distinguish the many chicken varieties.

SELF-COLOURED (OR SELF) AND SPLASHED

Feathers that have no markings – or hardly any markings – are called self-coloured or self. The self colours are the basic colours, such as black, white, lavender-grey, buff (a yellowish-brown, and a very popular colour in Orpingtons) and blue. In chickens, this last colour is, in fact, a dilution of black, and appears to the eye as a greyish-blue colour. The blue colour is passed down intermediately, that is, when blue is bred to blue, only about half of the chicks born will have their parent's colour, while the rest will have colour defects: they will be black, or white with small, irregularly-shaped, dark blotches. This white variant is called splashed. If the splashed chicken is mated with a black one, all of their chicks will be blue.

BUFF ORPINGTON

An example of barred feathers on this Plymouth Rock

Barneveleder showing laced pattern

BARRED FEATHERS

Barred feathers have alternating transverse markings – stripes running across the width of the feather – in two distinct colours. A good example of this type of feather pattern can be seen on the Amrock and Plymouth Rock breeds.

CUCKOO OR CREOLE STRIPING

The colour pattern known as cuckoo, or creole, is where the colour black has receded into transverse stripes, so that dark-grey and light-grey stripes alternate on the same feather.

LACED FEATHERS

Laced feathers have a border of a different colour all the way around the edge. Breeds with laced feathers include Barnevelders and the fabulous Sebright Bantams that look like stained-glass windows. Some breeds have been developed with double-laced feathers, where there is a second lacing within the feather, and there is a wide range of colour combinations, ranging from golden-blue laced through yellow-white laced to lemon-black laced and silver-blue laced, with the first colour indicating the feather's body colour, and the second, the colour of the lacing.

PENCILLED FEATHERS

Pencilled-feather markings include several types of lines or markings and are found in a whole range of old country-fowl breeds. Pencilled feathers take their name from the markings on the hen, the striking features of which are numerous little black spots on the feathers of the breast, back and wing shoulders. Between two and five pairs of spots are always found on either side of the feather shaft. The number and shape of these spots can vary from breed to breed: Frisians have tiny spots that are separate from each other, while in the Brackel, the spots are joined up across the feather's shaft, forming small transverse bars (this is sometimes called triple laced).

PORCELAIN, SPANGLED AND HALF-MOON SPANGLED

The basic feature of porcelain feathers is three colours, with the main, or ground, colour being a brownish-yellow or bay. At the tip of the feather is a large, rounded, black spot that is known as the spangle, and inside this spot, right at the tip of the feather, is a small, round, white speck, often called the pearl. In the porcelain, the bay ground colour and the black spangle can be replaced by other colours: if the normally black spangle is blue, then this is called blue porcelain; if the basic brownish-yellow colour is replaced with white, it's known as silver porcelain. Spangled birds have similar feathers to those with porcelain feathers, except that the pearl is lacking, but there is also a variant called half-moon spangled, where the spangles are not neat and round in shape, but more of a crescent. In all varieties, there is a wide range of colour options, ranging from silver black spangled to yellow white spangled.

COLUMBIAN, BELTED AND BLACK-TAILED WHITE

The Columbian marking was once called ermine, and, like the noble fur, it has a basic colour of white, with black markings at the body's extremities: the tail feathers are black and the hackle feathers are white, with black lacing. When there is so much black colour in the hackles that it appears almost solid, this is known as belted marking, as seen in breeds like the Lakenvelder. Birds with entirely white necks and black tail feathers are called black-tailed white. In all of the variations, the parts that are normally white can also be a golden-yellow– as seen in a buff Columbian or a golden belted, for example – and the black markings can be replaced by blue ones.

QUAIL COLOUR

The quail colour is the typical colour of the Belgian chicken breeds, such as the Antwerp Belgian, Bassette and Brabaconne, and the quail-coloured cock bird has a beautiful golden-auburn hue, with near-black hackles and a black tail, while the saddle feathers are a deep, velvety black, with golden-brown lacing. New colour combinations mean that the golden-brown can be replaced with either white or lemon-yellow, and the black markings, with blue, white or lavender. So it's possible to have blue quail, silver quail or lavender-silver quail.

PARTRIDGE, PARTRIDGE-MOTTLED AND WHEATEN

The markings and basic colour of the partridge type of chicken and its variants are the closest to those of the wild red jungle fowl (*Gallus gallus*) of South East Asia and northern India. Although called partridge, the colouring is that of the stereotypical rooster, with pitch-black breast and tail feathers; vivid orange-red hackles and saddle; rich, brilliant-red wing bows and back; and a glossy, greenish-black bar

LAKENVELDER COCKEREL   BROWN LEGHORN ROOSTER IN AUSTRALIA

orange-red hackles and saddle; rich, brilliant-red wing bows and back; and a glossy, greenish-black bar running across the wings. Look at, perhaps, a partridge-coloured Leghorn cock of the Dutch–German type, and you'll instantly recognise him as such: his female companions, however, are less spectacular. Breeding can also introduce a range of colours (blue or silver partridge, for example), and a mottling factor, where there are small, white flecks on the feathers. Wheaten is the colour pattern produced by selectively breeding out the black markings on the neck and saddle in both sexes; the peppering in the female (little, greyish-black dots sprinkled over her bay-coloured feathers) is also eliminated. In the wheaten, there are also colour variants, when the eliminated black may be replaced by blue, lavender, white or even cuckoo (see above, page 29).

SILVER-NECKED AND BIRCHEN

Think of the silver-necked pattern and colouration as being a 'reverse Columbian': the parts that are white in a Columbian (see above, page 30) are black here. But the tail and neck have no white markings, and the tail colour is similar to the ground colour: black. The markings are therefore only to be found in the neck feathers, where the black feathers are laced with thin, white edges. The shoulders and saddle of the cock are silvery-white (hence 'silver-necked'), but there is a further variation: when the black breast feathers are laced with silvery-white, it is called birchen. Once again, a range of colour variations is possible: where the white is replaced with a golden-yellow colour, you get golden birchen and golden-necked; replace the black with blue, and you have blue golden-necked and blue birchen.

chicken basics

TOP : CHICK COLOUR IS NOT AN INDICATOR OF THE ADULT COLOUR.

MIDDLE : THE BEAUTIFUL ORNAMENTAL COLOURS OF A COCKEREL

BOTTOM : SPECTACULAR POLISH POMPOM!

COLOUR, SEX AND AGE

The colours of birds are related to their sex and to their age: the appearance of chicks in their first and second feathering is very different to that of their adult plumage. Chicks of many of the colour varieties frequently have white in their feathering, which often only disappears entirely after their second moult, and juvenile cocks look remarkably like hens until they have developed their mature plumage. Likewise, when some patterns of birds age – such as porcelain and mottled varieties – their white spots seem to become bigger and more numerous after every annual moult. Buff- and blue-hued birds also seem to fade in colour during the year: this is due to the effects of weather rather than age because after the moult, their new feathers are as bright as a new penny.

ORNAMENTAL FEATHERS IN COCKS

It's the male cock birds that have the ornamental feathers, or 'sex' feathers. These are found around their necks and shoulders, and on their backs and saddles, and as well as having a soft texture, they are long, narrow and shiny. On each side of the cock's tail are the main sickles that protrude beyond the tail feathers in a lovely arc. In addition to the main sickles, there are the lesser sickles, a number of short and narrow sickles covering the tail feathers.

CREST, BEARDS AND MUFFS

Erect feathers on top of a cock's head are called a crest (or a topknot or tuft). On cocks, the feathers are the same shape as the hackles – long and narrow – while hens have shorter, broader feathers. Some breeds have fabulous pompoms, and the Poland has one so large that the bird can only see when looking forwards (you have to speak to it to let it know that you are there, otherwise it gets a shock); this pompom is also very high maintenance, needing washing and drying by the owner! Others have tassels, or narrow tufts. Under their beaks, chickens can also have beards; bearded breeds generally have no wattles (see above, page 23), or else very small ones, while some breeds have side whiskers called muffs or muffles. And both the cocks and hens of the Orloff breed (one of the few to have originated in Russia) have full beards and bushy 'eyebrows'!

CHAPTER THREE

Getting started

Before you start keeping chickens for their eggs or to raise them for the table, you will need to prepare well in advance for their arrival. This doesn't only mean preparing to meet their physical needs with a chicken house, nesting boxes, runs, feeders and so on – all of which must be in place before your chickens come home to roost – it also means brushing up on your knowledge of chickens so that you understand what you will be taking on. While some chicken breeds do make terrific pets, remember that, just as with any other animal, you are responsible for their health and well-being. Like cats, dogs and goldfish, chickens need daily care, and that means every day, so you must be prepared for this responsibility. If you are planning to go away on holiday, for example, you will need to consider who will look after your chickens while you're gone because there's no poultry equivalent of a boarding kennel or cattery.

Before rushing out and buying or building a henhouse and acquiring some birds, check the deeds of your house because those of many new-builds do not allow you to keep livestock, and even those of some older houses have similar exclusion clauses. If you are a tenant or leaseholder, you may need your landlord's or the freeholder's permission to keep chickens. Be sensible, too: if you live in a flat, keeping a pair of even one of the smallest breeds on a balcony is not a good idea – in fact, it's downright cruel, and you could find yourself in court facing charges for breaching animal welfare regulations. If your deeds or lease allow it, the next step is to check with your local authority to see whether there are any regulations that prohibit chicken-keeping in your area. In addition, depending on the size of your

proposed set-up, you may need planning permission to construct or install a large henhouse.

Generally, there are few legal restrictions or prohibitions on households keeping a small number of birds. Any restrictions that are in place are usually designed to stop people from establishing full-scale chicken farms in their back gardens. However, if you do have the space and plan on keeping more than fifty birds, then you are legally required in Britain to register your flock with the Department for the Environment and Rural Affairs (DEFRA). Anyone with just a few birds is also encouraged to register: registering means that you will be notified by text message if there is any outbreak of sickness that would require bio-security measures. In other countries, different registration requirements are in place, so check with your state or national poultry club, your local veterinarian, and, in the USA, the State Veterinary Service. If you have an allotment, don't assume that you can keep chickens on it as you may not be allowed to keep livestock, so check the rules and regulations and ask permission before starting to keep chickens there or else risk you and your flock being evicted from the site.

It's also important to speak to your neighbours: tell them your plans, how many birds you intend to keep, how large their henhouse will be and also where it will be located. Note that you don't need to keep a cock bird with your flock (hens will lay eggs without them) unless you are intending to breed

from it or just want one for a pet. Be warned, too, that your neighbours may object to a loudly crowing cockerel, and that you could then find yourself subject to a noise-abatement order, so take this into
account before acquiring one. (You'll find more information on cocks and crowing in Chapter 4, on
chicken behaviour, pages 59 to 60.)

You'll also need sturdy fencing to keep your chickens inside your property because not only do you not
want them scratching up your neighbour's garden, but in many countries there are legal requirements
for chicken-owners to protect other people's property from their livestock. Taking the environmental-
health aspect into account, you must also be prepared to keep rats, mice and other vermin under control through the use of traps or poison. Remember that shutting your chickens up for the night doesn't
mean that they are safe from attack. In both rural and (increasingly) urban areas, you must be prepared
to keep foxes and, sadly, human predators, at bay, none of which are nocturnal. Indeed, fox attacks during the day may occur particularly in spring, when foxes have hungry cubs to feed, and again in autumn, when they are teaching their offspring to hunt.

ALWAYS BUY FROM A REPUTABLE BREEDER.

YOU WOULD BE BEST ADVISED TO BUY YOUR COCK BIRDS FROM A DIFFERENT SOURCE TO YOUR HENS, TO AVOID INBREEDING.

As a result of the increased popularity of self-sufficiency and growing one's own produce, there are now many dedicated magazines and websites offering information on chicken breeds and their care and maintenance, as well as carrying advertising paid for by suppliers of henhouses, feed and birds themselves. Many of these magazines include listings for breed-suppliers, but remember that although a magazine may carry such ads, this does not necessarily imply 'official' endorsement. And on reading these ads, you may think that they've been written in a secret code, with DO, POL, HE and RIR being just a few examples of the abbreviations commonly used. These aren't codes, however, just shorthand ways of squeezing information into small adverts. For the record, DO means 'day-old'; POL means 'point of lay'; HE means 'hatching eggs'; and RIR stands for Rhode Island Red.

Birds are often sold as trios (one cock and two hens), and a numerical code is sometimes used to describe exactly what's on offer. In such instances, the breed name and sometimes colour of the birds may be followed by a pair of numbers: 1–2 means one cock and two hens; 1–0 means a single cock; and 0–3 means no cock, but three hens. At the end of the line will be another number – this is the date of the year in which the birds were hatched, and shouldn't be confused with the number of birds for sale. So, for example, an advertisement might offer: 'RIR 0–10 + Dorking Silver Grey 1–2 avail. '08'. This translates as ten Rhode Island Red hens plus three silver-grey-coloured Dorkings – one cock and two hens – that were bred in the year 2008. The trio of a cock and two hens is the breeder's method of getting rid of surplus cocks: they may not have the time, space or feed to raise all of their cocks to table weight. But be warned: these trios are almost always from the same brood, and so, at the very least, will be half-brothers and

the chicken keeper's handbook

Where to buy your chickens

sisters, meaning that they should be avoided to guard against inbreeding. Ideally, you should buy your cocks from a different breeder entirely in order to introduce new blood into the line.

A reputable seller will be pleased to talk you through the code, and by reading the chapter on the different chicken breeds in this book (see Chapter 7, pages 134 to 172), you'll be able to spot which birds are the ones that you want. Research each of the breeds using books, magazines and the internet, and find out about the appearance and characteristics of each to help you to be certain that you are getting the one that you want. Decide, too, whether you want a cock bird, as well as hens. There are also some rare breeds and exotics that may take your fancy, and you may find yourself being more interested in breeding and showing these birds than in keeping them for their utility. All in all, make sure that you do your homework before buying your birds, whichever breed of chicken you decide on, and for whatever reasons you choose to keep them.

Joining a local poultry club, or even just asking its members for their recommendations, will prove very useful if you are a first-time chicken-keeper, as will visiting a poultry show where you can familiarise yourself with the various breeds and meet their owners. Do some research beforehand, check out the various suppliers in your area and ask an experienced poultry-keeper to accompany you if you feel that you need help. Once again, a reputable breeder or supplier should be happy to help a novice keeper: it's in their (business) interests to do so. Remember that while they will not sell you diseased or otherwise defective chickens, it's unlikely that they will part with their finest birds because they will want to keep these for breeding – the birds that are offered to you will be fine if you want them simply for laying eggs, but they won't be show birds.

If having a good supply of eggs for your table is your primary objective, then don't overlook former battery hens. Battery hens are at the peak of their egg-laying life at just over one year old; after that, they are of no use to the battery-farmer and will therefore be 'discarded' and replaced by younger models. This does not have to be the end for former battery hens, however, and you can get them from commercial farms quite cheaply – or else from rescue organisations and charities – and if you then feed them a good diet, you'll be rewarded with a plentiful supply of eggs. The hens will inevitably be hybrids (which are famed for their egg-laying capabilities), so if you're not fussy about breeds, are primarily interested in eggs and want give a new home to a poor bird, battery hens are ideal. Don't be alarmed by their initial appearance: they will probably be bald and very nervous (you would be, too, if you had just spent a year in close confinement!) Plenty of tender loving care, rest, fresh air, good food and a little time will have them plucking up the courage to explore their new home, and they will soon grow a fine new set of feathers. They will continue to lay, albeit not quite as intensively, but that's the whole point of rehoming them.

Rehoming battery hens can be rewarding.

the chicken keeper's handbook

Where not to buy your chickens!

Although fewer live animals are being offered for sale at markets and fairs nowadays, it does still happen, and be warned that purchasing any animal at one of these is a risky business. Unlike when visiting a breeder or supplier, at a fair or market you can't see how the birds have been reared, and in what conditions, and you won't get a full picture of their overall well-being. Furthermore, if something goes wrong with your purchase, there's little chance of putting it right. Many sellers of chickens at markets sell surplus birds from fanciers and breeders, but unless it has had its leg or wing banded with a sealed band showing its year of birth, you usually won't be able to tell how old a bird is. Also up for sale are typically the bad layers: hens that are consistently broody or that are generally not up to scratch in some way. In many instances, birds from different breeders are housed together, which also means that there is a risk of disease transmission. In addition, a market trader may well exploit a novice's lack of knowledge. Simply asking for some chickens is not enough: you will need to be able to make a distinction between cocks and hens, and to know how to recognise young birds (if you

want them), lest you are fobbed off with older ones. To be absolutely on the safe side, only purchase your birds from a reputable supplier, a bonus being that a good supplier will be only too happy to encourage newcomers to poultry-keeping and to share his or her knowledge and advice with you.

You may also see advertisements in newspapers offering chickens for free; most of the time these will be cocks, but laying hens will sometimes be on offer. In such cases, be a little suspicious, especially of those that claim that the birds are a year old. A flock for free may sound enticing, but flags up some caveats: laying hens are at their peak of production at a year old, so why are they being given away? Most of the time, they will turn out to be much older, and perhaps past their laying best. You also need to consider whether these birds could be sick or diseased (healthy-looking birds can still harbour lice or scaly-leg mites). If you are relatively new to chicken-keeping, you may not be able to tell whether the birds are healthy or not. And if you already have chickens and want to increase your flock, there is a danger that the free

UNLESS YOU BUY FROM A REPUTABLE SOURCE, YOU WILL HAVE NO IDEA OF THE HISTORY OR WELLBEING OF YOUR CHICKEN.

A SHOW OR FAIR MAY BE AN IDEAL PLACE TO BUY CHICKENS.

birds will import disease into your henhouse and infect your existing chickens. The main reason why birds are offered for free is because they are no longer of any use to their owner. And unless you know the owner and know that they have a genuine and valid reason for wanting to get rid of their birds – perhaps they are relocating or find keeping the chickens too difficult – then it's best to avoid free birds.

When to buy your chickens

Many surplus birds are sold at bona-fide poultry shows, and poultry clubs often organise sales. The best time to buy chickens is in early spring, when the majority of birds on offer will be around a year old and in peak condition for either breeding or laying eggs. And autumn sales may include older birds that may be past their peak in the show ring, but that are still capable of producing fine, strong chicks or plentiful eggs. But note that it does make sense at autumn sales to buy stock that was hatched that spring; these chickens can be kept as adults and should lay (albeit sporadically) throughout the winter before really getting into their stride the following spring.

If you're not buying at spring or autumn sales, then you need to select the best birds on offer. Remember that chicks and young birds grow quickly, especially during the warm summer months' long days of sunshine, when there's also plenty of fresh grass.

THE NUMBER OF CHICKENS TO BUY DEPENDS ON SEVERAL FACTORS – THE SPACE YOU HAVE, AND WHETHER YOU SIMPLY WANT EGGS, OR TO BREED.

THE BEST AGE TO BUY HENS IS AT 'POINT OF LAY', AROUND TWENTY WEEKS OF AGE. THEY WILL BE MORE EXPENSIVE, BUT THE BREEDER WILL HAVE DONE THE HARD WORK OF REARING THEM, SO THEY ARE EASIER TO CARE FOR.

How many chickens should you buy?

The number of hens (and cocks) you keep should depend on a number of factors, including the amount of space you have available; what you want the birds for (egg production maybe, or meat production, breeding or showing); and the breed. Many poultry-keepers suggest that if you want only a couple of hens, you should plan on having three birds: chickens are sociable animals, so if one dies, there's two left to keep each other company.

If you simply want eggs for your table, ask yourself how many eggs you eat, as well as how many you can eat. You may think that having lovely fresh eggs every day will encourage you to eat more of them, but even the greatest egg-lover can tire of eggs after a bit! Work out how many eggs you use a week now (including for baking), and then add on another 50 per cent to cover increased consumption and storage later on in the year when the birds are moulting (see below, page 69) and not laying. From four hens, you'll probably get three eggs a day. Four to six hens will probably provide more than enough eggs for the average family, with some left over to give to neighbours and friends. Also remember that overcrowding birds leads to aggression and illness (which can be triggered by stress), and that your aim should be to keep your birds in a happy state, not in battery-farm conditions.

The age to buy chickens

If you want your chickens' eggs fertilising, then one rooster per six hens should ensure success, but this may vary from breed to breed: in the case of heavy breeds, like the Brahma or Cochin, one cock will service three to five hens, while you can increase the number of hens to eight or ten for the light breeds. If serious breeding is your aim, then you'll need more than one cock, but be warned that even when they have their own harem there can be problems with aggression, and that in some cases, cock birds will fight to the death. To breed birds successfully, you'll need space – and plenty of it – to ensure that the cocks can avoid each other.

Earlier in this chapter, rescued battery hens were suggested as an option for a flock of laying hens. These birds will be more than a year old, and possibly eighteen months of age. But not everyone will feel confident enough to take on a near-bald flock of hens who'll take a while to settle in before starting laying, so if egg production is your primary intention, the best age to buy hens is at point of lay (often abbreviated to POL). This is usually around twenty weeks of age, after the supplier has done the hard work of rearing the bird. Although hens will be more expensive at POL, they will be ready to begin their productive life. However, even though they will be at the point of beginning to lay, the upheaval of moving to a new home will delay the start of their egg production by two weeks or so, until they are nicely relaxed and settled in. Note, though, that some of the heritage breeds, as well as some of the dual-purpose breeds (for eggs and table), may take much longer to start laying – and sometimes even six months.

Younger birds are less expensive than POL hens, but you'll have to bring them on, that is, feed, house and care for them until they start laying eggs. Many suppliers are happy to sell young birds – after all, it saves them the time, money and energy required to raise them to POL. The average chicken bred for the production of eggs will, from chick to layer, consume about 6.8 kg (15 lb) of feed, and some of the more slowly maturing, heavier breeds can eat twice that amount before they begin producing eggs. Young hens aged between eight and twenty weeks of age are called pullets.

Day-old chicks may look cute and fluffy, but they are really for the more experienced keeper because you'll need either bantam hens to act as surrogate mothers or powered 'brooders' in which to raise these chicks that have been hatched through artificial incubation. There are some further problems with day-old chicks: firstly, their mortality rate is high. Many suppliers offer day-old chicks by mail order, and if the transit time is just a few hours, then the chicks can generate enough body heat to keep warm. But even if they are sent in insulated boxes, delays in transit can mean that you take delivery of dead, dying or seriously stressed and weakened chicks. Even if their new owners collect the chicks themselves, once home, many of the chicks may not survive. Secondly, it is almost impossible to tell the sex of a bird when it's this young. This means that there's probably a 50:50 ratio of males and female birds in any group of day-old chicks that you buy, so that if you want hens only for laying, you will still be feeding and rearing unproductive male birds until they are identifiable as such, and then you'll have to think about what you want to do with all of the surplus-to-requirement cockerels. In short, if you are new to chicken-keeping, don't be tempted to buy day-old chicks.

BELOW: PULLETS, LIKE THESE BANTAMS, ARE OFTEN CHEAPER TO BUY, BUT REQUIRE MORE CARE, SO MAY NOT BE IDEAL FOR FIRST-TIME CHICKEN-KEEPERS.

BELOW: NEWBORN CHICKS MAY BE CUTE, BUT THEY REQUIRE A GREAT DEAL OF CARE AND ATTENTION TO SUCCESSFULLY RAISE THEM, AND ARE BEST LEFT TO EXPERIENCED POULTRY OWNERS.

It is possible to buy chickens that are even younger than day-old chicks in the form of fertile eggs. Again, you need to be equipped to deal with these by having surrogate bantam 'mothers', who will turn broody and will then sit on and hatch the eggs. Using fertile eggs is, however, a good method if you want to raise pure-bred chickens and adult birds are either not available or too expensive to purchase. But this is only something that you should consider doing when you have experience and knowledge of chicken-keeping and, furthermore, of the needs and characteristics of your chosen breed.

If you are intending to breed, then hens a little over a year old and just past their first moult are the best choice since they have proved themselves to be solid and strong, having already been through the processes of laying and moulting.

What to look for in a chicken

While many chicken-owners insist on the advantages of one breed or another, in truth, the best chicken is a healthy chicken. By buying your birds from a reputable dealer or from a club or society member or sale, you can be reasonably confident that you are getting well-kept and healthy birds. It's very useful to be able to spot problems by looking for tell-tales signs on a bird, though, and here are some useful tips.

CHECK ALL THE CHICKENS LOOK
HEALTHY AND ACTIVE.

WHEN HANDLING THE CHICKEN, IT
SHOULD FEEL FIRM AND WELL COVERED.
IT SHOULD NOT FEEL BONY.

A HEALTHY CHICKEN SHOULD HAVE
BRIGHT EYES AND A CLEAR NOSE.

- Look at the floor of the pen: the faeces that you see there should be firm, well formed and partly white in colour. Slimy, watery, green or yellow diarrhoea-like droppings are a sign of ill-health in chickens.
- Look for a bright, active bird with a good car riage or posture, not one that is drooping or hunched.
- Handle the bird. It should feel firm for its size, and there should be a reasonable covering of flesh on both sides of its breastbone. Remember that although light breeds will be less well cov ered in this region, the breastbone should never stick out or feel too prominent. Instead, it should feel like the blade of a knife, with no flesh on ei ther side.
- A chicken's eyes should appear bright and bold. Inspect both eyes and check that the colour of their irises match. Also check that both pupils are evenly shaped and that they do not seem to blend into the iris.
- Look at the chicken's nostrils – there should be no sign of mucus. Hold the bird and gently press the side of each nostril to check for any mucus. If you are unsure whether there is any, place your ear on the chicken's back and have a listen; there should be no hint of any wheezing or puffing.
- Check that the sinuses, which are located just above the nostrils, are not swollen or puffy.
- Look into the ears. There should be no sign of any cheesy-looking substance (this is a sure sign of infection).

- A chicken's comb should be bright in colour, waxy-looking and not shrunken or shrivelled. A purple comb may indicate circulation problems and generally poor health. (But be aware that some breeds have naturally darker-coloured combs, so make sure that you are familiar with the particular breed's appearance and characteristics.

  Note that a hen's comb colour can also change when she is brooding chicks or is moulting and not laying.)
- Look at the chicken's legs and run your hands down the shanks. They should feel smooth, with no raised scales and no rough or crusty yellow patches.
- Look at the chicken's bottom. The feathers around the vent area should be clean and there should be no sign of diarrhoea. Dirt around this area may also indicate the presence of parasites like fleas, lice and mites. (Although tiny, these are visible to the naked eye, but if you feel happier using a magnifying glass to inspect this area, then do so.)
- Look under the bird's wings and remember that the under-part, nearest the body (roughly equivalent to the human armpit), is a favourite hiding place for mites. Lift up each wing, gently brush the feathers in the opposite direction to that of their growth and look carefully for any movement indicating the presence of fleas, lice or mites.
- The bird's plumage should be shiny and full-looking. If, during the summer, you find that the plumage on the backs and necks of some females in a breeding pen is broken, it has probably been caused by the mating cock.
- Check the crests and beards of birds that have them for any evidence of northern fowl mites lurking in there. (See Chapter 9, page 210.)
- With regard to a breeding cock, remember that he must come from good-quality breeding stock and be of the type outlined in the breed standards. He should be firm to handle and well muscled. Look at his eyes: the colour should be bold and even and should surround a perfectly black pupil. His legs and feet should be clean and strong (he needs them to be in order to be able to mount and mate with hens). His comb should conform to the breed requirements. His age is important: while a cockerel is sexually mature at around six months old, it is better to select a bird that was bred during the previous spring or early summer.

Handling and transporting chickens

You will need to pick up your chickens from time to time, usually in order to inspect them at close quarters and to move them. Picking up a chicken for the first time can be quite strange. First of all, though, you have to catch it! Try putting down some food and luring the chicken towards you. Don't handle your birds roughly because this causes them stress and may even damage them physically. This is the best way to pick up a bird:

- start by placing one hand over the top of the bird to stop it from flapping its wings;
- now place your other hand underneath the bird, positioning your middle finger between its legs;
- use the fingers on either side of your middle finger to hold the bird until it stops wriggling around – you can use your thumb and little finger to hold the tips of the wings still;
- keep a firm, but gentle, hold on the bird as you lift it;
- rest the bird's keel (breastbone) on your forearm, close to your body; this makes the bird feel more secure (many hens actually love being held in this position) and less prone to wriggle around.

Before setting out to get your birds, make sure that you have the henhouse and run, feeders and water containers, nest boxes and perches ready for their arrival. It's also a good idea to ask the breeder or supplier what type of foodstuffs the birds have been given so that you can buy the same style or brand for them and continue using it. Alternatively, you could ask to buy some of the suppliers' feed to take home with the birds so that you can gradually introduce a different type of food into their diet.

Ideally, you should have proper poultry crates or baskets in which to transport your birds. (This is especially important if you are buying birds at a public sale, where animal-welfare officers are in attendance because they will insist that your carrying box conforms to any government legislation regarding the transportation of livestock.) In most instances, though, a good, strong, dry cardboard box with plenty of air holes and a decent lid to prevent escapes will suffice. Cover the base of the box or carrier with hay or straw to give the birds a better grip and stop them from sliding around inside. If you have found a reputable local supplier, then the birds' journey should now be as short, comfortable and stress-free as possible.

the chicken keeper's handbook

Settling your chickens into their new home

When you get home, keep the chickens confined within their house for a few hours – or overnight – so that they can calm down and get used to their new home. If you will be allowing your birds to range free, keep them shut in for twenty-four hours before letting them out to roam. Once they have settled, lift the pop-hole and let them explore their run. Don't push or shoo them out into the run – let them make their own way out so that they don't become disoriented.

Now start to get acquainted with your chickens. Move slowly and spend some time crouching down by the feeder. Hunger and curiosity will ensure that the birds soon approach you, and before you know it, they'll associate you with food and you'll have them eating out of the palm of your hand. Some chickens become used to routine sights and sounds: if, for example, you wear the same shoes when feeding and inspecting them, they'll become accustomed to seeing them and you, and will be less nervous about being handled. They also get used to voices, songs or calls – for feeding and for bedtime – so don't be alarmed if, every time the birds see you or hear your voice, they come running to you, hoping for a tasty treat.

GET TO KNOW YOUR CHICKENS.

CHAPTER FOUR
Chicken behaviour

Understanding chicken behaviour will help you to understand your birds' basic needs and to ensure that their environment is well suited to their lives. Pretty much all chickens behave in the same way, but some breeds – and many individual birds – have particular characteristics. Some hens, for example, become very attached to special 'secret' places in which to lay their eggs, and there are some (usually those living in small flocks of three or four) who can only lay their eggs when being stroked or when seated on their owner's lap – or both! Much chicken behaviour is routine, so by understanding it, you will be able to recognise anything out of the ordinary as a sign that there's something wrong with either an individual bird or the flock, such as the presence of a predator. And understanding when a bird or flock is alarmed or distressed will enable you to take the necessary steps to restore calm.

UNDERSTANDING WHY A CHICKEN IS ALARMED
OR NERVOUS WILL HELP YOU CALM IT.

FEEDING TIME IS A GOOD TIME TO SEE THE PECKING ORDER IN PLAY.

MAKE SURE YOUR CHICKENS HAVE ENOUGH SPACE. OVERCROWDING CAN CAUSE PROBLEMS.

The pecking order

Chickens are outgoing, gregarious birds who live in flocks, and the harmony of the group is maintained by a hierarchy – the pecking order – that governs where each individual chicken stands within it. The hierarchy begins with the top bird, the most dominant hen, who is usually the oldest (and sometimes the most aggressive) bird in the flock. Other birds will defer and give way to her at the feeding trough. The dominant hen can peck at any individual below her, as can the next in line (who, however, cannot peck the bird above her in the hierarchy). The dominance of one bird over the one below carries on until it reaches the end of the line, and the last bird can be picked on by them all.

The pecking-order system works well, and once it has been established, harmony will reign within a flock. But introducing a new bird can set feathers flying, and the new hen may be the victim of bullying. The first hen to spot the newcomer will issue a single warning croak to alert the rest of the flock, and in the wild, the flock would then chase off the newcomer. There's nowhere really for new birds to run to in the case of a domestic flock, however, so they are often bullied until accepted into the pecking order.

HENPECKING: CHICKEN BULLYING

Adding more than one hen at a time to a flock can help to prevent bullying, but it's a good idea to introduce the birds to each other gradually by first housing them in separate enclosures so that they can see each other and get used to each other's presence. Keeping the new arrivals separate is also important when it comes to the birds' health: the newcomers may be carrying some illness with them, and

keeping them apart from your existing birds for a few days will allow you to monitor their health. When the quarantine period is over and the birds have become familiar with one another, the new arrivals can then be integrated into the existing flock.

When the chickens finally meet, it's best to arrange for this to happen in an open space, so that the new-comers have room to escape if they feel threatened; providing plenty of hiding spaces and extra perches around the run can also help. Chickens living in cramped or overcrowded conditions are more like to resort to bullying behaviour, so make sure that your birds have plenty of space.

Introducing the new birds at night can also help to prevent them from being henpecked because the other hens will be too sleepy to bother! Removing the dominant hen, placing her in a new environment where the newcomers have already established themselves and then returning them all to the main flock can also work. Don't, however, be tempted to put the hen at the bottom of the pecking order in a pen with smaller hens thinking that this may boost her confidence. More often than not, she'll turn into a complete tyrant and overwhelming bully to demonstrate her new, 'superior' status.

If a hen is being bullied, the other birds will be pulling out her feathers, and they will also attack her vent until it's sore and bleeding. The victim needs to be taken away from the bullies and given her own space, with food and water, where she can recover overnight. Suitable spaces include a cardboard box or cat transporter brought indoors into a cool environment, such as a shed, outhouse or garage (as long as it is safe from predators). If you don't fence your hens in full time, she could be placed in the pen alone while the others run free during the day. Alternatively, you may have to fence off a section of your garden with chicken wire for her as a temporary daytime measure.

A NEW FLOCK OF CHICKENS MAY NEED HELP UNDER-
STANDING WHERE THEY SHOULD GO!

NEW CHICKENS WILL PERCH ANYWHERE IF YOU DON
GUIDE THEM

A new flock

If there is no established flock with a pecking order already in place – for example, if you are bringing your first chickens to their new home and there aren't any old hands to show them what to do – you may find that your newcomers behave remarkably stupidly. They may not realise that they have to go into their house at night to roost on the perches that you have gone to the trouble of providing for them, for example. Instead, they may flap about and try to reach a tree's branches or else sit on the roof of the henhouse or shed (it'll always be just that bit out of arm's reach). In this case, the only thing to do is to gather them all up, carry them into their house and put them on the perches. Then keep on doing this until they learn to do it for themselves. Be prepared, however, for one bird who just seems to like human attention and the routine of being put to bed in this way. (If you have a small flock, you'll soon get to know the character of each chicken, and their individual preferences.)

Cocks and crowing

Technically speaking, a cockerel is a male bird who hasn't yet had his first adult moult (this takes place when he's around eighteen months old), after which he's called a cock. Traditionally, a cock bird is the lord and master of his flock, who protects his hens and fertilises the eggs to create the next generation. He also spends much of his time strutting around and crowing.

YOU MAY FIND THE MALES OF SOME OF THE HEAVIER BREEDS ARE QUITE PLACID AND FRIENDLY – SUCH AS THE RHODE ISLAND RED.

KEEPING A COCK WITH YOUR HENS IS A GOOD WAY TO PREVENT BULLYING.

Many chicken-keepers like to keep a cock bird as a pet, but the cocks of some breeds can be more aggressive than others, so if you have small children, it's a good idea to avoid the more ill-tempered ones. The males of some of the heavier breeds, such as Maran, Orpington, Plymouth Rock, Rhode Island Red and Sussex, not only make handsome 'garden accessories', but are also placid and friendly birds. Brahmas and Cochins are very heavy birds, but while they make terrific pets, they may be too big for children who want to carry them. Faverolles, Silkies and Wyandottes are all non-aggressive birds, especially with children.

One of the advantages of keeping a cock is that he tends to prevent bullying among hens – he is, after all, lord and master of his poultry kingdom. But remember, you don't need a cock if you only want eggs from your chickens because hens will still lay eggs without one. If you want fertilised eggs for breeding and increasing the size of your flock, however, then you will need a cock to fertilise the eggs.

Some downsides of keeping a cock are that he doesn't produce eggs, and that egg production can be lowered if the hens are stressed by his amorous attentions (he can be quite rough with the hens, with his spurs and claws tugging at their feathers and him pulling on their head feathers as he holds on to them).

From a human's point of view, the main problem with cocks is their crowing. All breeds of chicken crow, and some of the smaller breeds actually have the loudest voices, while some of the bigger breeds have a more pleasant-sounding vocalisation. Before crowing, cocks will flap their wings to announce to their flock – and to any other bird who happens to be looking at them – that they are fit, strong, handsome and in charge. Like other songbirds, cocks crow at dawn – this can be very early in the morning during the summer – and they'll continue to crow throughout the day, as well as at dusk, when they call the hens home. If you are really unlucky, you'll have a cock that crows in the moonlight; when a neighbour's light comes on; and every time that a car's headlights move past his line of sight. His song may sound very pleasant to the owner, but it can be a nightmare for the neighbours. Additionally, cocks will crow in defence, in challenge, and to announce the 'all-clear' to signal that any danger has passed. (Such danger may take the form of other birds, predators and humans. Newspaper-, milk- and postal-delivery people will inevitably set a cock crowing, as will the sound of another cock crowing, in which case you can expect a battling duet.)

The only way to stop a cock from crowing at dawn is to remove him to a darkened box at night, to place that somewhere dark, confined and safe, and then to release him only at a suitable hour of daylight. A wooden wind chime or 'baffles' of bamboo planted around the perimeter of the run can also help to prevent the noise from travelling by creating a knocking or rustling sound that makes the cock's crowing seem less loud in comparison.

Although there are historical reports of hens moulting their female plumage, growing male feathers and then crowing, probably as the result of a hormonal imbalance, hens don't crow. They do, however, emit a soft, growling sound when they are broody; cackle proudly to announce that they have laid an egg; and make a 'took-took-took' sound when they are calling their chicks to come and feed (cocks also make this noise when calling hens to feed). Hens will screech loudly when alarmed, and will also make a 'burring' sound to warn others of any dangerous birds overhead before running as fast as they can to the safety of the henhouse. (Don't be alarmed if your new flock is alarmed by its first sight of laundry flapping on a clothesline, by the way: your chickens will soon become used to your routine, just as you'll become used to their routines and sounds.)

the chicken keeper's handbook

Courting chickens

When a cock calls the hens to feed with his 'took-took-took' song, he's hoping that the notion of a tasty treat will bring his 'girls' around him. The hens know that food isn't usually the only thing on his mind, for many cocks use it as a lure to tempt hens into mating. If a hen accepts the food, the cock will then strut around her with one wing dropped before attempting to mate with her. If she is in lay, or is approaching lay, and is prepared to accept his amorous advances, she will squat down and allow the mating to take place. When a hen is not in lay, however, she'll take the treat and will then make a swift exit.

During the spring and summer breeding seasons, some cocks can become quite aggressive, and will peck at your feet (this many not be a problem for adults, but a belligerent bird flapping around and pecking at their toes may frighten small children). Once the human has walked away, the cock thinks that he has won and will start crowing to tell the world of his magnificent victory. When you pass the cock again, he will attack again. It's the most aggressive birds that are the most virile and fertile, so unless you need them for breeding, cocks that are overly belligerent are best despatched to the cooking pot. (Note, however, that an aggressive cock may well calm down once the breeding season has passed.) Alternatively, to avoid running the gauntlet of his belligerence every time you meet, you could keep a breeding cock in an enclosure that you don't have to enter very often. And if you need to catch an aggressive cock, do this by throwing a coat or cape over him as he approaches, and then pin him to the ground under the coat.

Egg-eating

Whatever you feed your hens, never give them eggs: if you do, they'll find out just how tasty they are and will eat what they lay! (And note that a clever, but sneaky, domestic cat likes nothing better than a warm, freshly laid egg as a breakfast treat.)

DURING BREEDING SEASONS, COCKS CAN BECOME AGGRESSIVE.

EGG EATING CAN BE A PROBLEM IF YOU DO NOT COLLECT EGGS FREQUENTLY.

A BROODY CHICKEN WILL ATTEMPT TO HATCH EGGS EVEN IF THERE IS NO COCK AROUND.

Collecting eggs on a regular basis usually curbs the problem of hens eating eggs, but what usually happens is that no sooner has one laid an egg, than one of her girlfriends will pounce on it, peck it open and eat the contents. The real problem is that egg-eating is behaviour that is soon copied by other hens, so you'll need to intervene quickly and find the culprit. Keep a close watch on the hencoop, listen for that telltale 'I've laid an egg' cackle, try to identify which hen is to blame for any egg-eating and then take her out of the pen as soon as possible.

If you can't identify the guilty hen, there are some other methods that you can try. First of all, make sure that the entrance to the nest box is in the darkest part of the henhouse and facing away from any window (the darkness makes it hard for hens to see the eggs). You can also make the nest box itself darker by hanging a fringe of fabric – effectively a fringed curtain – over its entrance. Next,

ensure that the wood-shavings in the nest boxes are always at least 9 cm (3½ in) deep; fluffing them up will let the eggs sink into the shavings so that they are hidden from sight. Now place a layer of fluffed-up hay on top of the shavings to make a soft, comfortable laying bed. Finally, leave a few fake eggs around the chicken run. These need to be solid and quite heavy, and you can buy ceramic or rubber ones from agricultural suppliers (note that even the most stupid hen isn't fooled by a golf ball)! With luck, the egg-eating hen should then peck away at a fake egg for a while, get bored and then give up the practice, all the while leaving the real eggs alone.

If the egg-eating continues, then the final solution is to install roll-away nest-box liners in your nesting boxes. Commercially available (and not too expensive), these ensure that as soon as an egg is laid, it rolls gently to safety to await collection later.

the chicken keeper's handbook

Broodiness

A BROODY HEN WILL OFTEN NEST IN AN
OUT-OF-THE-WAY PLACE!

Hens can become broody in late spring and early summer – even if there's no cock around – and when they do, they will sit on eggs in an attempt to hatch them. Some breeds are broodier than others, and will flatly refuse to leave the nest, getting mighty annoyed if you try to lift them out; and as soon as your back is turned, these broody hens will make straight for the nest to resume their position. Birds sit on their eggs for twenty-one days, so a broody hen will sit on unfertilised eggs for all of this time – and when nothing happens, she'll sit some more, in so doing, effectively barring the other hens from the nesting box.

The main way to stop broodiness is to collect all newly eggs laid promptly, because if she has no eggs to sit on, a hen is less likely to become broody. However, if you do have a broody hen, you could separate her from the other birds by putting her in her own house, but with a slatted or wire floor and no nest box. This will make it uncomfortable for her to squat down, and she should soon tire of trying to be motherly. Note, though, that this method does tend to put a hen off laying for a while, so it may be ten days to two weeks before she starts to lay again.

With free-range birds, you'll have to keep a careful eye on the hens for signs of broodiness. It's not uncommon for them to take up positions in large plant pots, under hedges or (speaking from experience) in baskets of clothes pegs! Furthermore, if you find that your free-ranging hens are laying eggs outside, rather than in the cosy nesting boxes that you have thoughtfully provided for them, try keeping them in their run until mid-morning, by which time they should have finished laying. That said, some hens have remarkable holding power, and will wait until they are let out and can visit their favourite laying spot. You'll then have to be quite cloak-and-dagger in your spying: the hen will know that you are watching her, and will stay away from the spot until she thinks that you've turned your back.

Fair weather for fowl

Chickens are pretty robust creatures, and are quite hardy in cold temperatures, but they hate wind and snow, and look as though they've been pulled through a hedge backwards in the rain. Don't expect hens to be in much of a mood for laying eggs during the winter either: light is crucial for their egg production, so short days have an impact on them.

If your chickens are kept in a run, then they must be provided with shelter from the wind and rain. If they roam free in your garden, they'll usually find their own shelter: under a bush, perhaps, or, more likely, sitting in the porch or doorway on your back doorstep. On cold days, it's also vital that you constantly check that their water supply has not frozen. And to prevent any exposed flesh from being frost-bitten, you could rub a little petroleum jelly on to their combs for protection.

CHICKENS NEED TO BE ABLE TO TAKE SHELTER IN BAD WEATHER.

Great escapes

You can give a chicken plenty of space in your back garden in which to roam and it will still decide to go off and explore next door. This wanderlust is probably the origin of all of those 'Why did the chicken cross the road?' jokes, the answer being simply 'To get to the other side'. Chickens will exploit any hole in a fence, gap in a hedge or weak spot in a chicken-wire barrier that you didn't even know was there. They may look nice and plump, but they can still squeeze themselves through quite small spaces.

Most of the time, their escapades will lead them to your kitchen door: they will have become used to seeing you emerge from here, will therefore associate the kitchen with food, and will consequently congregate on the back doorstep waiting to be fed. At other times, individual birds may get bees in their bonnets and just must travel; in such cases, you'll need to check the primary feathers on the chicken's wings Although it sounds horrible, clipping a chicken's wing does not hurt or harm the bird in any way. It's simply a method to ensure that 'flighty birds'- especially those that free roam- stay close to home. All you have to do it trim the tips off the main flight feathers on one wing only: trimming one side makes the bird's flight 'lopsided' and makes it flutter in a circle rather than a straight line. The tips of the flight feathers on one wing are trimmed about 5 cm (2 in) but you must use the quill colour as your guide (cut too much off and the ends will bleed) so only ever trim the feathers where the quill is white. Post-moult, a chicken will have grown fine, new feathers, and will need to have her wings clipped afresh, but if she's already been clipped, then keep an eye on her and try to find out how she's escaping. Usually, she will return home of her own volition when it starts to get dark, but until then, she will be vulnerable to attack from foxes and dogs, and to traffic, too.

Note that some breeds fly better than others: heavy and fancy breeds tend to be pretty earth-bound, and a fence about 1 m (around 3 ft) high will usually be enough to restrict their movement.

Sometimes chickens like to explore.

CHICKENS MOULT EACH YEAR.

The magic moult

Each year, chickens lose their feathers. When you see it for the first time, it can come as a huge shock because on opening the henhouse door, you'll find that it's full of feathers. Your first thought may be 'Fox attack!', but then a head count may reveal that all of your chickens are safe. Then you may see that one, or more, of your lovely birds is balding… Be assured that this moult is perfectly natural (and so is your likely reaction, even when you know that this will happen!)

The shock of the moult is really down to the fact that there's no specific time of year when it occurs: it all depends on when the individual bird was hatched. And it can be hard to watch a bird in moult in deep winter, when chickens really need their feathers for insulation and warmth. Birds moult in sequence: first to go are the neck and upper-back feathers, followed by those on the breast; next up are the fluffy 'trousers' or 'petticoats', and, finally, the back and tail feathers. A young, healthy bird will take around six weeks over her moult; an older hen can take up to three months to refeather. The first signs that the feathers are growing back is when you see tiny clumps emerging from the 'tubes' at the back of the chicken's neck.

At the first sign of the moult, some poultry-farmers remove the hens' feed for twenty-four hours to speed it up, or switch them to a less nutritious feed, before moving them on to a power-packed, concentrated feed to provide the nutrition that will enable a hen to regrow her feathers. If you don't want to speed things up, it's still worth feeding a moulting bird a dietary supplement to give her a boost. (These are readily available from feed-suppliers.)

CHAPTER FIVE
Housing chickens

In theory, chickens are perfectly capable of looking after themselves, which means foraging for food, perching on low branches of trees and shrubs and making nests in secluded corners. However, in all but the warmest climates, chickens need shelter: although they are hardy creatures, they hate wind and rain and dislike being wet and muddy. Chickens furthermore need protecting from predators: the main threat is the fox, which will kill all of the chickens in a henhouse, even if it only takes one away to eat. Rats, dogs, badgers, stoats and birds of prey, such as hawks and owls, can also pose a significant threat to chickens. And rather than you having to wander around for ages seeking out those secret egg-laying sites, it's a lot more convenient if your chickens lay their eggs in one place. All of this means that you'll need to provide your birds with a henhouse.

It's important to remember that although having chickens wandering around the garden is fun, their health and well-being is your responsibility, and that while keeping them is not labour-intensive, you should be prepared to provide your birds with daily and routine attention. Besides food and water – see Chapter 6, pages 105 to 133 – the two basic requirements for your chickens are shelter and space, and these must be in place prior to their arrival. So do not buy any birds until you have made the necessary preparations to house them.

the chicken keeper's handbook

Henhouses

Chickens need somewhere to roost at night. This is not only for their own comfort, in order to keep them out of the cold, wind and rain (chickens are not 'waterproof', like ducks!), but to give them protection. A secure, dry and well-ventilated henhouse is therefore essential, and there is a wide range of options open to the chicken-keeper. You could, for example, convert an existing shed or outhouse; build your own (and there are plenty of plans and designs available to download for free from websites); or you could buy a henhouse. You could opt for a traditional design, or for something ultra-modern; you could pay very little (perhaps if you buy a second-hand henhouse) or a great deal – as prices vary, so does quality. Some henhouses are supplied with runs attached, while others are designed so that you can allow your birds to range freely; alternatively, you could build your own permanent run. Whatever you choose will depend on your circumstances.

More importantly, the henhouse must be suited to your birds' needs: it must be the right size for your flock; it must be weatherproof and sturdy; and it must allow you easy access to the inside for purposes of egg-collection and cleaning.

LOCATION

Before even considering a style or design of henhouse, you need to think about exactly where it is going to be located. Spare a thought for your neighbours: they may not want a view of a henhouse from their windows, or would it be placed too close to property boundaries? The size of the henhouse is also important: ideally, it should be as large as you can afford (if you are purchasing one or constructing your own), and certainly as large as your space allows. Overcrowding chickens must be avoided as this causes bullying, stress and illness.

Note that wherever possible, the front of the henhouse should face south-east, especially during the winter, so that the chickens – who like to be warm, but can't take full-on sunshine all day – get the benefit of the sun in the mornings, while the front is nicely shaded at the hottest time of day. Draughts are a disaster for chickens, so place the henhouse in a sheltered spot out of the path of prevailing winds and away from any frost pockets. Choose a well-drained spot, too, because chickens can't cope with wet, boggy ground.

SECOND-HAND HOMES

If you are tempted to buy a second-hand henhouse – and these can be real bargains – first ask why it's for sale. If the owner says that it's because a fox got in, then inspect the henhouse carefully to see where the fox gained entry before deciding whether or not to buy it.

Remember that any second-hand housing must be cleaned thoroughly before use, even if it hasn't been lived in for some time (the eggs of mites and bacteria may still be present). Creosote, the number-one eradicator of hidden dangers, is not available for domestic use, but can still be purchased for agricultural use. So give the henhouse a good coating of creosote inside and out, paying particular attention to nooks, crannies, joints and overlapping wood. Then allow the house to dry thoroughly and let the fumes clear before letting your chickens anywhere near it. If you can't get creosote, then a really good scrub with a strong disinfectant like Jeyes Fluid, followed by a rinse-off with clean water and a final rinse with a 50:50 solution of white-wine vinegar and water, will work. Note that vinegar is a very effective cleaner and disinfectant (and inexpensive, too), which won't harm your chickens. Used undiluted, it's also effective against E. coli and salmonella, so it's useful to keep a bottle to hand for cleaning, and for a final rinse of your own hands after handling or cleaning the chickens and their house.

THE ARK IS A POPULAR HENHOUSE STYLE

SIZE MATTERS

There are many sizes of henhouse available. If you are buying a new one, be wary of manufacturers' statements regarding the number or type of birds that their particular product will house because such figures are generally based on both roosting capacity and 'commercial layers', which are small-bodied, Leghorn-type birds, not the larger breeds. These figures don't always take account of birds' requirements – the placement of feeders or run size, for example – while the quoted size will also usually be for birds that are kept on a free-range basis. If your birds are to be confined to a run, then they will end up spending more time in the henhouse, especially in bad weather, as they won't be able to shelter under hedges or in trees. On those days when your birds will be staying inside, they'll need enough space in which to scratch around and feed, as well as to avoid those above them in the pecking order. So it's a good idea to look at the bird-housing number adver-tised by the manufacturer and then to divide it in half. A good measure is at least 30 cm^2 (12 in^2) of floor space per bird

Dust-bathing is vital for chickens as the dust helps them to keep themselves parasite-free, and birds furthermore really seem to enjoy it, which means that a sheltered area is also important for keeping the dust-bath dry.

HENHOUSE DESIGNS

If you decide to make or buy a henhouse, you can choose from a range of possible shapes and designs, ranging from the simple to the highly elaborate. There are square, rectangular and triangular henhouses; there are two-storey versions; and there are some built on stilts that the chickens reach by means of a removable ramp. Although this last option means that the birds are well off the ground and safe from foxes, they are also a bit out of the reach of humans, and the henhouse can be difficult to clean if you have to stand on a ladder. Many henhouses are raised off the ground, even if it is only by a few inches, either on legs or on wooden skids. A dry floor is vital, and raising the henhouse off the ground ensures that the base stays dry; protects it from rot caused by resting directly on damp earth; and discourages vermin attack.

HUTCHES FOR HENS

The type of henhouse that you will need will be determined by the number and type of chickens that you want to keep, and by how much space you have available. Small bantams need significantly less overall space than heavy breeds, and it's quite possible to convert a large rabbit hutch raised on legs into a henhouse for a few birds: one-third of the wooden-floored hutch becomes the roosting and nesting area, while the remaining two-thirds are floorless, giving the chickens access

to fresh grass. You could make a little ramp or gangplank leading up to the pop-hole (see below, page 85) for the chickens to access between the two spaces. Since only the front of the run section is covered in wire, the 'hen hutch' is almost completely wind- and waterproof. The only drawback with this type of accommodation is that hutches often have a hinged roof opening, which can make for a difficult – if not backbreaking – job when it comes to cleaning out the henhouse. So if you are considering a top-opening henhouse, first check that you can reach into it easily – and that the lid doesn't slam down on your head every time you open it! Alternatively, opt for a model whose entire roof slides open on runners.

ARKS

Henhouses constructed in a triangular shape are both very easy to build and require few materials. Called an ark, this shape was originally used to stop sheep from jumping on it. Although it is a

nice, traditional design (and effective against sheep), this shape has a number of drawbacks and does not make the most ideal chicken accommodation. For instance, in arks, the apex, or pitched roof, becomes low at the eaves, which always means that there is a large proportion of unused and unusable space beneath, and that there's often not enough room for the birds to perch comfortably. On the positive side, arks are easy to move: many are designed with handles at each end so that two people can lift and move the structure to a new site in the garden. And if you are a lone chicken-keeper, you can buy arks on wheels, making moving them even easier.

THE EGLU

If you are thinking of keeping a couple of hens – and no more than three birds – in your garden to provide a few eggs, then it's worth considering an eglu. An eglu is a small henhouse, with integrated nesting and roosting areas made out of insulated polymer, and many versions have runs already attached. The attached run has upward-turning base panels that prevent foxes from digging their way in. The entire structure can be dismantled quickly and easily for cleaning and disinfecting, and it is lightweight, so you can move it around the garden to give the chickens a new patch of fresh ground every two or three days. While they are not the cheapest option for housing three hens, their innovative design, small size and bright colours have made eglus very popular with urban chicken-keepers who want a few eggs for their breakfast. And they retain their value should you decide to sell it on if you later increase the size of your flock; alternatively, you could use a spare eglu as a broody coop and chick run if you decide to raise young chickens from eggs.

the chicken keeper's handbook

Back-yard chickens

Arks, converted hutches and eglus mean that even if you live in a town, you can still keep chickens as semi-free-range birds, simply by making sure that your yard or garden is entirely enclosed by chicken wire to keep the chickens in and predators out. However, you should never believe that semi- or wholly free-ranging chickens are entirely safe from fox attacks, and it is vital that your chickens are housed safely at night.

If you are out at work all day, then you really need to consider having a run – an enclosed area outside the henhouse where the chickens can run around, scratch about and take the air. Don't be fooled into thinking that letting your birds roam free for an hour or two before you leave will work. Although you can teach them to come back if you rattle some scratch corn in a bucket (they'll soon learn that that's the sound of a treat), they also have minds of their own, and sometimes no amount of coaxing and cajoling will entice them back when you have to get to work on time.

Movable or permanent housing?

When you are deciding what type of henhouse is best for you, one of your considerations should be whether to have a movable or a permanently sited structure. While arks, eglus and hutch conversions are ideal for three or so chickens, larger numbers will require a bigger henhouse, and you'll need to decide whether it's going to be moved around or will remain in the same spot permanently.

During the nineteenth century, when the Victorians went mad for chickens, many of those who could afford them made a feature of their henhouses, in much the same way that dovecotes became must-have garden ornaments. At this time, henhouses took the form of a lean-to built alongside the wall of a garden or stable block. The shed and run generally both had roofs, and separate doors allowed access to either the house or the run. If you have a suitable wall (but not one that forms part of your own home or your neighbour's house), then you could construct a variation on this. Such runs originally had compacted-earth floors, with straw or dried bracken spread over them (you could instead use silver or sharp sand, but make sure that it's not builder's sand), with grain sprinkled into it so that the birds could root around for food. This would be ideal for chicken breeds that have legs or feet that are thickly covered in feathers.

MOVABLE HOUSING: THE FOLD METHOD

The fold method of movable housing comprises a small house with a larger run attached to it. A small fold can house around six hens, making it ideal for the chicken-keeper with only a small space, while bigger houses will accommodate around thirty birds. It is easy to manage and maintain, and is effective against foxes and other predators. The chickens are completely enclosed within the unit, and, like the smaller ark, it can be lifted using poles or handles or moved around on wheels. After a few days in the same spot, and once the ground underneath the unit has been grazed, pecked and generally scratched up by the chickens, the unit can be moved one length along the garden. Moving it regularly prevents overgrazing and allows the last grazed area to recover while the unit is rotated around the garden.

When the unit is moved on to a new spot, the soil on the previous patch needs to be raked over; if necessary, you may have to reseed sparsely grassed areas with grass seed (and a mixture of grass seeds, including clover, rye-grass, fescue and meadow grass, will make a nice mix that will keep the chickens very happy when it has grown). An annual application of lime where the chickens have grazed is a good idea: this will kill off any parasites that could contaminate the chickens, as well as helping the grass to grow. Note that the base or floor of the sheltered part of the fold needs to be very strong because it will be in contact with the ground; it also needs to be regularly inspected for holes or rot and kept in good repair.

PERMANENT HOUSING: A CONVERTED SHED

Instead of buying a commercially produced henhouse, you could always adapt an existing outhouse or shed. An existing shed could easily be converted into a henhouse: a 2 x 1.2 m (6 x 4 ft) shed, with two sturdy perches fitted lengthways and a good-sized outside run, will easily accommodate eight large birds. The advantage of a shed is that sheds have human-sized doors that allow you to enter without stooping, and you can get a wheelbarrow in as well, which is handy when it comes to cleaning. Most of the time, too, sheds are already fitted with a lock, which all henhouses should have to deter thieves. You can also customise sheds to make them appear less utilitarian and more decorative, although this would only be for your benefit, of course, and not the chickens'!

Most sheds have at least one window; ideally, this should be covered with a grille or netting to prevent the glass from being broken – a broken window is a danger not only because the birds could cut themselves, but because it allows predators free access. If the window faces into the run, it's worth removing the glass completely, covering it with wire mesh, and adding some shutters that can be opened during the day to let in plenty of fresh air and light and can then be securely closed again at night. (If the run is secure, the shutters could be left slightly ajar at night in very warm weather.)

Don't position your converted shed so that the window faces due south (otherwise it may become overheated), or into prevailing winds (where it will get blasted or become rain-soaked). Note that a sloping roof is better than a flat one, on which rainwater or snow may collect and cause leaks, and that an eaves gutter should be installed to drain off rain.

Insulation

It's important to ensure that there are no holes and crevices in the henhouse's structure – particularly if you are using a shed – that would allow your birds to escape or ingress by vermin. Although wooden sheds are pretty strong, they still need treating with a suitable preserver against rot. In addition, in order to accommodate your chickens in comfort, you may need to add some insulation to the inside walls and then cover it with hardboard or plywood (make sure that this is made with a water- and-boil-proof glue, and look for the letters 'WSB' stamped or printed on to the boards). If you use foam insulating sheets, note that these must be covered, otherwise the chickens will peck at them and eat them! Insulation stops the temperature inside the henhouse from dropping too much: if the temperature within drops below -12° C (10.4°F), egg production will fall by around 25 per cent; and if the temperature falls below –17°C (1.4°F), egg production will cease. Similarly, hens become unhappy when the temperature rises above 26°C (78.8°F), and egg production will also be affected if night-time temperatures are high.

NICELY INSULATED MODERN HENHOUSE   MESH WINDW VENTILATION

Old stone or brick outhouses are pretty well insulated from both cold and heat and have the advantage of brick or concrete floors, which makes them (almost) vermin-proof and easy to clean.

Ventilation

Although the henhouse needs to be well insulated against the cold, it also requires fresh air, but not so much that it causes draughts (which can be fatal to chickens) or significantly lowers temperatures. Without adequate ventilation, a henhouse will soon become stuffy, damp and unhygienic – ammonia from droppings will build up – and it will then provide the perfect breeding ground for respiratory problems in your chickens.

Ventilation can either take the form of a window covered in mesh or be provided by specially designed grilles and air holes. These should be located near the top of the henhouse so that the stale, warm air rises and escapes.

Lighting and heating

Another advantage of using an existing shed as a henhouse is that sheds are often already equipped with electricity, or at least electric lighting. If not, then it's a good idea to install an electric cable with which to provide artificial light – this is not only so that you can see into every nook and cranny for cleaning thoroughly, but you can also use it to lengthen the hours of 'daylight' for your chickens during the long winter months, so that they continue to lay. You could also plug in a plate-warmer or heating pad because when there is a frost, the small amount of heat that this will emit will be enough to stop the birds' drinking water from freezing.

YOUNG PULLETS BENEFIT FROM A WARMING LIGHT.   POP-HOLES

There's no need to heat the henhouse, however, because your chickens' feathers will keep them warm, and they also tend to snuggle up together at night and tuck their heads into their plumage. In fact, heating their henhouse would mean that your chickens would be subjected to a great shock when going outside in the morning. Their wattles and combs would be in danger of freezing, too, and they could develop a chill and then die.

Pop-holes

Pop-holes are the openings by which chickens enter and leave their house. Ideally, these should be 20–60 cm (8–23 in) above ground level and furnished with a gangplank so that the chickens can get in and out. All you need for a gangplank is some good-quality wood, with small wooden slats every 10 cm (4 in) across it, and with no sharp edges or splinters that could injure the birds' legs, firmly anchored or secured into place so that it doesn't move. Pop-holes prevent draughts blowing along henhouse floors, and while the perfect size of a pop-hole will depend on the size of your chickens, on average, they are about 30 cm (12 in) wide and 40 cm (18 in) high (but if you keep crested fowl, you may need to make them taller to accommodate those head feathers!) The pop-holes shouldn't be so small that the chickens have to stoop down to get through them because they may scrape their backs.

Vertically sliding pop-hole doors are recommended because hinged doors can slam shut, trapping birds inside or outside, while horizontally sliding runners may become befouled and blocked with debris, so that they stop sliding properly. It's a good idea to be able to shut the pop-hole doors from a position outside the run's wire mesh – a piece of string or a chain works well (and I know one chicken-keeper who can open and shut his henhouse's pop-holes from the comfort of his kitchen, using an ingenious winding mechanism). You can also get timer mechanisms that will automatically open the pop-holes in the morning; these are useful if you have a full-time job with regular hours because you can shut the pop-holes on your return and reset the timer for the next day. (But don't assume that your chickens will be safe if you spend an hour or so at the pub after work: closing the pop-holes at sunset is vital in order to keep the birds safe from foxes and vermin, so if you are not prepared to come home to put the chickens safely to roost, then you need to reconsider whether you should be keeping them at all.)

The floor: solid or slatted?

Cement, tiled and brick-laid floors significantly reduce the number of rats and mice that can access the inside of a henhouse – and they are easy to clean. Don't forget that the birds will need a dust-bath, though (see below, page 94). In a permanently sited henhouse or converted outhouse or shed, a solid floor like this is the best option, but with a moveable house, it is out of the question.

Slatted floors are useful in that they allow droppings to fall through the slats; when the henhouse is moved, the ground underneath can then be cleaned. The big problem with slatted floors is that they are not predator-proof: foxes can get under the henhouses and can then bite the chickens' feet. A floor made of fine wire mesh works well in both permanent and movable houses: these allow the passage of droppings through the mesh, which can then be collected on a board or tray positioned below. A compacted-dirt floor is the most primitive solution; this can quickly turn to mud and is the hardest to keep clean and disease-free. A solid, good-quality wooden floor works the best: most chickens prefer to stand on a solid floor rather than on a slatted one. But note that the droppings will eventually rot the wood – and can also make it very slippery – so you will need to maintain it regularly. Also be aware that rodents will eventually chew through the wood to gain access.

The floor: litter

The floor of your henhouse will need to be furnished with 'litter' for bedding, and for the chickens to root about in. Clean sharp or silver sand (not builder's sand) or dust-free softwood- or pine-shavings are all suitable materials for this.

Hay is not recommended, however, because it tends to become twisted around the chickens' legs, when it may stop the circulation of their blood, and it also tends to clump and cake when droppings fall onto it. It can furthermore make birds crop-bound (see crop impaction, pages 220 to 221). Straw is fine, but it should be chopped up so that it's not too long, and you'll need to make sure that it's fluffed up regularly to keep it aerated and dry (it can hold moisture and become stale and mouldy). You can aerate the litter with a rake, but if you scatter some grain for the birds into it, they will turn it over as they root around for the food. If you use straw or wood-shavings, note that they cause much more dust than sharp sand, so wear a facemask when raking or cleaning out the henhouse to avoid inhaling any particles.

A GOOD WOODEN FLOOR IS IDEAL - BUT DOES NEED MAINTENANCE.

Wood-shavings make the best litter: they neutralise ammonia and dry out manure, making it easier to handle. They can be bought from agricultural suppliers in compressed bales, and you can also use shavings acquired direct from sawmills (but note that these shavings won't necessarily be kiln-dried, making them less effective at absorbing moisture; they may also contain hardwood shavings, which turn dark when damp, causing your litter to appear 'mottled').

In addition to wood-shavings, hemp-based products are becoming increasingly popular. These are more absorbent than wood-shavings, and have the advantage of settling down more quickly. You can add this litter to a compost heap, but remember that chickens must not have access to the compost heap for health and hygiene reasons, so make sure that it is fenced off from them. Shredded newspaper is also available in compressed bales, and this makes very good bedding: it's soft, absorbent, contains no parasites and can easily be burned after use. The only downside is that it's so lightweight that gusts of wind can blow it around. Autumn leaves make a nice addition to the litter, and chickens like scratching around in them, but note that they must be absolutely dry because mould can cause respiratory problems in chickens.

The litter in the henhouse needs to be about 15 cm (6 in) deep, and should be raked over every day, when matted portions – such as under perches and around water drinkers – should be removed. If you have droppings boards (see below, pages 92 to 94), the litter should stay fresh for about four to five months; it should be replaced completely every five to six months. (Your nose will tell you when it needs to be changed as the smell of ammonia, dampness or general mustiness is unmistakable.)

Nesting boxes

Nesting boxes are vital for hens: if you don't provide a suitable spot in which they can lay their eggs in comfort, they will wander off to find a place of their own. Laying an egg takes a little time, too: on average, a hen will be busy laying for about 1½–2 hours a day, so the nesting boxes must be comfortable and large enough for the birds.

Nesting boxes don't have to be elaborate confections, but they do need to be smooth, with as few joints as possible, so that mites can't hide in, and infest, any cracks. Sturdy pieces of cardboard or cardboard boxes cut down to size are ideal materials for nesting boxes: they're inexpensive, warm, and have soft edges, and when they are worn out, or become infested by fleas or mites, you can just burn them on a bonfire and replace them with fresh cardboard.

Nest boxes should be situated inside the henhouse. Ideally, there should be one box for every three laying birds, and each box should measure around 45 cm (15 in) high and 30 cm^2 (12 in^2).

A DEEP LAYER OF STRAW WILL PROVIDE COMFORT FOR YOUR HENS.

This size will suit most light breeds of hens, but for smaller bantams, the boxes could be a little smaller, and for larger breeds, a bit bigger. Nesting boxes are enclosed on three sides, the front 'door' entrance being open, as is the top of the box. If you want to cover the top of the nesting box, then it's best to do so with a lid that's on a steep slant to prevent the hens from sitting on the top and covering it with their droppings.

Nesting boxes should be situated just off the ground (if you have to position them higher, then you'll need to provide perches for your chickens so that they can hop into the nest boxes from there) and in the darkest part of the henhouse because hens like to lay their eggs in a quiet, dimly lit place (under the window is a good spot, so that the morning sunlight shines on their backs and not in their faces). If you are installing several nesting boxes, don't place them all at the same level: chickens will use the box that they think is situated in the best position – that is, in the dimmest and most secluded part of the henhouse – and you may find that they all try to lay their eggs in the same box, which may lead to eggs getting stamped on. A hessian or sackcloth curtain – or else an old, clean tea towel cut to size – hung across the front of the nest box will provide a sense of quiet seclusion for the hens, who seem to like pushing past it, and appear to derive a sense of security from it apparently 'closing' behind them.

Line the nesting boxes with a deep layer of straw or hay (the nesting box is the one place in a henhouse where hay can be used). Note that this must be cleared out regularly, and the boxes dusted with louse-killing powder to keep them free of infestation. Sprinkling a little grit into the nesting boxes amid the straw is also useful: the hens can have a little nibble while they nest, and this grit also contains the calcium required to make the shells of hens' eggs. Remember to collect your chickens' eggs every day and to remove any broken eggs to discourage egg-eating (see above, pages 63 to 64, for more on this) because once this habit starts, it's difficult to crack (no pun intended!)

Remember that it's infinitely more convenient to collect eggs from the outside of the henhouse via a door or hatch than from the inside. This is not so much of a problem if your henhouse is a shed, or has a lift-off lid, but it's otherwise worth investing in a henhouse that has nesting boxes that are accessible from the outside. These may be a little more expensive to buy, but it means that you won't have to enter the house itself and disturb any birds inside while they are laying. Because it's easier to reach the eggs, this type of design also encourages regular and routine egg-collection, and keeps potential egg-eating to a minimum.

New birds will occasionally try to roost for the night in nesting boxes. This is to be discouraged, otherwise you will end up with befouled nests and dirty eggs. So when introducing new chickens to your henhouse, prevent them from roosting in the nesting boxes by covering the front of the boxes with a board or 'curtain', and the tops with a sloping lid. The newcomers will soon get the message, and will instead use their perches for roosting on at night.

NESTING BOXES SHOULD BE POSITIONED SO YOU HAVE EASY ACCESS TO THE EGGS.

Perches and droppings boards

One or two perches running the length of the hen-house will provide roosting places for your chickens at night. If there are two or more perches, they must be situated at the same height, otherwise the birds will all try to get on to the highest one and will squabble all night. The perches must also be situated well above ground level and higher than the nesting boxes, otherwise the chickens will sleep on them. Unless you are keeping long-tailed breeds (which require higher roosting points), position the perches about 30 cm (1 ft) above the ground. Note, however, that heavier breeds may find it a bit of a struggle to get up on to their perches at this height, may damage their muscles and tendons by repeatedly jumping down, and may then develop a painful foot condition known

as bumblefoot, so if you think it necessary, provide a gangplank to enable your birds to walk up to the perches. Because warm air rises, in winter, you could raise the perches by a few more inches so that the birds benefit from the additional warmth, but once again, make sure that they can access their perches easily (and get down from them easily, too).

It's a good idea to place removable droppings boards under the perches. About half of a chicken's manure is produced at night, and by using boards to catch the droppings, the litter stays cleaner for longer, and cleaning is made much faster and easier. The droppings contain high levels of ammonia, which is why the perches need to be situated above the floor, and why ventilation in the roof or upper sides of the henhouse is required. And to avoid them being contaminated by faeces, make sure that feeders and water containers are not situated under the perches. If you use removable droppings boards, you could set these

PERCHES SHOULD BE ROUNDED FOR COMFORT.

at the height suggested for the perches (see above), and then place the perches about 15 cm (6 in) above them.

The thickness of the perch is very important. Ideally, it should be at least 5 cm (2 in) wide and 3 cm (1 in) thick for bantams and small breeds, and 8 cm (3 in) wide and 5 cm (2 in) thick for larger breeds. Furthermore, the perches should not be square at their top edges, but should instead be slightly rounded off so that the birds' toes can grip them comfortably. Always used planed wood for perches, and never wood with bark attached: roughly sawed wood is full of splinters, and beneath the bark is the ideal home for parasites like red mites. In addition, both of the latter types of wood are difficult to scrape clean – which you will need to do when you clean the perches – and for that reason, too, you should not fix perches permanently to the walls of henhouses, but should instead set them into slots or brackets, or construct them as a free-standing frame, so that they can be removed for cleaning.

Allow at least 20 cm (8 in) of perching space for each bird – 30 cm (12 in) for larger breeds – and note that if a perch is being used that's longer than 1.8 m (6 ft), that this will have to be given additional support in the centre.

Dust-baths

Chickens have to wash themselves and keep mites at bay, and they do this by taking daily dust-baths. You will therefore need to provide your birds with a permanent – and completely dry – dust-bath that they can use all year round. This could consist of four posts hammered into the ground to a height of 60 cm (2 ft), with a roof over it and the soil underneath loosened up and mixed with dry sharp or silver sand, or even some ashes from a wood (but not coal) fire. The hens will soon get to work on it, but the most important thing is that it stays dry.

If the run is movable, then a shallow box (about 20 cm/8 in high) filled with sand, dry soil and ashes will do the job. To enhance the anti-parasitical qualities of the dust-bath, you could add a dash of diatomaceous earth to the mix. This is a fine, siliceous earth that is chiefly composed of the cell walls of diatoms (marine or fresh-water algae) and is used in filtration and as an abrasion. Your poultry-feed supplier should be able to provide you with it, and a handful added to the dust-bath will work against mite infestation. Once again, the size of box that you will need depends on the size of the chickens that will be using it: for small birds, like bantams, a box 60 x 60 cm (2 x 2 ft) will do; larger breeds need a bit more space in which to roll around, so increase the size to 1–1.10 m^2 (3–3½ ft^2). Fill the box with clean sand – you'll need to change this regularly – and then place it in a dry space. If the run isn't covered, during wet weather, move the dust-bath into the henhouse, so that the chickens can still have their daily 'bath'.

JST BATHS ENABLE CHICKENS TO KEEP FREE OF MITES. FREE-
NGE CHICKENS WILL CHOOSE THEIR OWN LOCATION!

LEFT: GREEN STUFF SOHULD BE HUNG FROM A RACK, RATHER THAN PUT ON THE FLOOR.
RIGHT: DRINKERS SHOULD BE ABOVE THE FLOOR, AT A COMFORTABLE HEIGHT FOR YOUR
CHICKENS TO REACH.

Free-ranging chickens will make their own dust-bath, which will typically be somewhere that you'd rather they didn't, like on top of a newly planted seedbed, so providing them with a ready-made dust-bath may prove useful if you want to save part of your garden from being scratched up. Be warned, however, that if you have a cat, it will probably use the hens' dust-bath as its toilet – just because it can!

Feeders and drinkers

Just as there are various styles of henhouses available, so there are many different types of feeders and drinkers, all of which have advantages and disadvantages. Note that thanks to the pecking-order hierarchy within a flock, one or two birds may hog the feeder, effectively blocking the other chickens' access to it, so in order to ensure that all of the birds get a square meal, two feeders are better than one. When it comes to feeders, if you only have a few hens, then a heavy, glazed-earthenware dish or large dog bowl will suffice. Ideally, it should have an inward-facing rim so that the feed doesn't spill out over the top, but never fill it up to the rim anyway. And if you want to buy a feeder, also look for an inward-facing rim, otherwise the chickens will scatter their feed all over the place, which not only encourages vermin, but the food will become contaminated by the birds' droppings. The feeder must be made of a material that's easy to clean, so don't be tempted by any pretty, folksy or ethnic looks because you'll need to be able to give it a good scrubbing, inside and out. Small feed hoppers or tube hoppers that are suspended from the roof of the henhouse (well away from the perches) are a good way of making sure that the birds don't scratch or sit (or worse) in their food. Make sure that such a feeder is suspended at the right height to enable the hens to reach their feed. Alternatively, stand the feeder on a sturdy, upturned box so that it's about 15 cm (6 in) off the floor, just below the chickens' throats: they'll be able to reach it easily, but its height will make it difficult for vermin to gain access to it.

In the case of feeders for green stuff, a rack or manger hanging up in the henhouse is recommended. Don't dump vegetable matter on the floor because this is unhygienic and attracts vermin, while lettuce leaves can be treacherously slippery! A manger or rack will also give the birds some diversion and exercise: jumping up a couple of inches to get at their fresh greens will keep them occupied.

Do not place drinkers on the ground or floor of the henhouse where they could be overturned (a wet patch of litter and no drinking water results), and remember that these, too, can become contaminated. The best option is probably either to suspend a reservoir or jar-type drinker or waterer from the roof or to place it on a shelf along the henhouse wall, in both instances at the right level to suit your birds' size. 'Little tons' or jar waterers are made of easy-to-clean plastic and are available in different sizes, from 0.5 l (½ pint) to 5 l (1 gall); the size that you need will correspond to the amount of water that your chickens drink within twenty-four hours. Check their water and water levels regularly; replace the water with a fresh supply every day; and make sure that their water hasn't frozen on very cold days.

Note that if you decide to keep birds with crests or beards, then you must provide them with special feeders and drinkers, the design of which should ensure that their feathers are not soiled or made wet when they feed and drink.

Make sure your run is secure, and suitable for the size of your flock.

Runs

In addition to their house, your chickens will require a run, which, like the henhouse itself, needs to be fox-proof. Two runs of a suitable size to accommodate your flock and their breed size are a good idea if you have the space: one run can be used as such, while the other is rested and its ground re-seeded to break any parasitic cycle.

Some henhouses come with runs attached, and if the house is small, you can move it, and the run, to a new patch of grass quite easily. Most often, the run is a netted wooden frame attached to the henhouse that is open to the elements on all sides, top, or roof, included. Note that if a chicken run is to be left without a roof, then it must be positioned at least 3 m (10 ft) away from any tall structure, such as a wall, the roof of a garage, shed or outhouse or a tree, because foxes can, and do, climb, and will use these as springboards from which to launch themselves into the run. So when you construct or set up your henhouse and run, try to think like a fox and look at the structure through vulpine eyes.

A run that has a solid roof is a better option, not least because the rain is kept off and the run's earth won't then turn to mud. This is not only best for 'feather-footed' breeds, but for all chickens, and especially for those that fly. Even though a wire fence about 1.8 m (6 ft) high will keep all birds safely inside – even the most flighty Anconas and Hamburghs – foxes can still climb up it and get in, so a solid roof also offers more protection from predators. Furthermore, it prevents wild birds from enter-

ing the run and feasting on chicken feed (and stops their droppings from fouling it, too), and if you have a cat, it can climb on to the roof to its heart's content without the chickens being disturbed by its presence (cats love nothing better than walking, sleeping and just 'bouncing' on the wire roofs of chicken runs – because they can!)

The same fencing and roofing considerations apply for permanently sited runs. And it's easy to construct your own run. In practice, the most commonly used chicken wire has a 19-gauge thickness and 5 cm (2 in) mesh and is 1.8 m (6 ft) tall. The fence posts should be about 4 m (12 ft) apart, and at least 30 cm (12 in) of the fencing wire needs to be dug into the ground all the way around the run to stop predators from digging their way in – and the chickens from pushing their way out. Permanently sited runs should ideally have a tiled or cement floor, with a layer of at least 20 cm (8 in) of sharp sand on top in which the chickens can root around. If you don't put in a solid floor, then make sure that the ground is well drained and, if possible, that the inside of the run is a bit higher than the outside as this will help to prevent water from running in.

If you build a gateway into your run, ensure that it's absolutely secure. Note that two sliding bolts at the top and bottom of the gate are better than one, and that a lock might unfortunately not go amiss either: foxes aren't the only predators that you have to guard against. Indeed, chickens are valued for both their egg-laying potential and meat, while rare or pure breeds and fancy show birds are also valuable to their owners, all of which means that two-legged thieves may need deterring. And just as you wouldn't want someone to steal your cat or dog, so you wouldn't want to lose your hens.

For all chickens, the ultimate run is the garden, and freedom to roam around in it. This works if you have enough space; are prepared to sacrifice your flowerbeds (unless they and any vegetable beds are fenced off); don't mind your chickens 'manuring' your garden; and they have a safe place in which to roost at night, and some nesting boxes, too. But only let your chickens roam free if your garden is completely enclosed by a wire fence, and, even then, if your neighbours don't mind the occasional visit. Free-range chickens will forage for insects, eat weeds, make their own dust-baths, and will generally be on the move all day, and getting plenty of exercise means that they won't grow fat, but will instead become lean (tasty) and healthy birds. The downsides are that they are very much at risk from hungry foxes and raptors, and that it can be hard to get them all back into the henhouse when you want to shut them up for the night. That said, if you feed them in their 'home base' in the evenings, they'll soon learn to come back pretty smartish, and sprinkling a very narrow trail of grain up through the pop-hole and into the henhouse can lure them in, too.

the chicken keeper's handbook

Cleaning and maintenance

Hygiene is very important when it comes to keeping chickens, and a fundamental rule is not to keep too many chickens in a small area: overpopulation not only causes stress, but infestations and disease spread more quickly, too. A second rule is that the henhouse, litter, nesting boxes, feeders, drinkers, perches, droppings boards and runs must all be routinely and scrupulously cleaned. Clean before – and not when – it becomes necessary, and you will go a long way towards keeping your flock healthy.

If you have a few hens that roam free, then you won't have so much cleaning to do (albeit possibly more tidying up in the garden) than if you keep them in an enclosed run. Nevertheless, and regardless of how many birds you have, you must do the following every day:

- gather the eggs;
- scrape the droppings boards clean and sprinkle them with fresh wood-shavings;
- clean out the feeders and drinkers;
- change the water;
- make a visual inspection of the house and any fencing and repair as required;
- ensure that you have provided sufficient feed and water for your birds, and a dust-bath;
- rake the litter in the henhouse and outside run area and collect and dispose of all of the droppings.

Remember to do the following every two to seven days:

- depending on the number of birds you have, scour the perches clean.

Every seven days, you should:

- scour the droppings boards with disinfectant;
- clean and disinfect the feeders and drinkers (white vinegar is good for doing this).

Every seven to ten days:

• if you have an eglu, ark or hutch or another type of henhouse with a movable run attached, check the condition of the ground under the henhouse and run and move to them to a new site if necessary.

Every ten to fourteen days:

• scour and disinfect the perches.

Once a month (or, in winter, every six weeks):

• disinfect the nesting boxes and put in fresh straw and grit.

Every four to five months:

• remove all of the litter from the henhouse (note that litter should feel dry to the touch; if it feels damp, then remove it);
• disinfect the floors and walls and then add new litter.

In addition to following the above regime, note that there are a few jobs that need doing on an annual basis:

• if an outside run is permanent, dig out the old layer of dirty sand and replace it with a new layer of clean sharp or silver sand, to a depth of at least 20 cm (8 in);
• whitewash the interior of your henhouse;
• treat wooden posts and any other wooden structures with preservative.

CHAPTER SIX
Feeding chickens

Chickens that roam free will feed on various foods. Chickens are omnivorous, and if they are allowed to roam free, they will happily feed on seeds, herbs, leaves, grubs and insects. Because fowl are natural foragers, it's their instinct to range around and search for food. And equipped as they are with full-colour vision and a highly developed sense of hearing, they are able to keep good track of the other members of their flock, even when ranging over wide areas. Modern, highly domesticated breeds still have the same desire to hunt for food, and enjoy scratching around for it. That said, you'll get the most out of your chickens if you feed (and water) them well and regularly because a poor diet that is low in minerals, vitamins and nutrients will lead to fewer eggs being laid and sickly birds. So even if they are free-ranging or in a fold that is regularly moved on to a new patch of ground for them to turn over, chickens still need two meals a day, ideally at the same time every day. The contents of these main meals can be readily bought from pet shops and agricultural suppliers, along with additional supplements of grain feed, some fresh 'green stuff' and grit (although not a food, this is vitally important for the birds' digestion and consequent absorption of nutrients). Your feeding regime must, however, be tailored to the breed and size of birds that you are keeping, their age, their environment and the 'products' for which you are raising them, i.e., for eggs or for meat.

Additive-free, GM-free and organic feeds

In order to maintain profitability, many commercial poultry farmers use a method called maximum feed-conversion efficiency: in other words, they raise their birds using the minimum amount of feed and time. To do so, the feed is often manipulated through the incorporation of low levels of antibiotics (known as coccidiostats) to control the single-cell protozoa that cause the disease coccidiosis, which seriously affects a chicken's intestines and can be fatal. (See Chapter 9, on pests, parasites and diseases, for more information on this and other problems.) Other compounds, including arsenic compound, are sometimes used to speed growth, while other additives include mould-preventatives and preservatives to stabilise the vitamins and minerals that are vulnerable to fluctuations in temperature and humidity. Such additives may have health implications for humans, and, along with animal-welfare issues, are among the main reasons why many people have turned to rearing their own laying hens and table birds.

While these additives may be necessary in order to produce healthy, viably commercial birds in large-scale chicken farms, clean, dry and well-ventilated housing, uncrowded conditions, access to fresh, clean water and uncontaminated feeding stations, as well as to natural daylight and pasture or grazing ground, may mean that the need for such additives can be avoided. Many feedstock companies do offer feeds without additives and genetic modification (GM), and the produce of organic-grain companies complies with strict standards (although these standards can, and do, vary from country to country). Organic and guaranteed-GM-free feeds do, however, cost more than regular feeds that still have the same nutritional values.

Basic dietary requirements

The basic dietary requirements for healthy chickens are water, protein, carbohydrates, vitamins, fats and minerals. These are all provided in readily available 'rations' that come in pellet, crumble, mash or scratch form, and that are prepared to suit the requirements of birds as egg-layers, table birds for eating or birds kept for raising chickens or for breeding for shows.

When you buy your birds, it's a good idea to ask the supplier which brand and type of food they have been given. Make sure that you then buy the right, familiar feed straightaway, so that as soon as your birds have been installed in their new home, they have their favourite food to hand – or beak! Having provided the birds with continuity when they moved into their new home, you can then make any adjustments and changes gradually over time. (Chickens are creatures of habit, so it's important not to chop and change feed types or feeding methods and regimes.) Begin feeding any new food to chickens in moderation because if their digestion is not used to it, it can cause uncomfortable scouring (diarrhoea), which can also be fatal. So start them off with small amounts and gradually increase the quantities that you give them over the following days.

MAKE SURE YOU GIVE YOUR CHICKENS FAMILIAR FOOD WHEN THEY FIRST ARRIVE WITH YOU.

Digestion

Understanding how chickens eat and digest their food is the first step in making sure that your birds are, in fact, eating – as well as in ascertaining whether they are eating too much or too little – and making use of the nutrients contained within their food. Chickens have a fairly simple, but remarkable, digestive system: because they don't have teeth, birds can't chew their food, and so require an internal digestive 'processor', and insoluble grit, in order to digest their food.

When a chicken feeds, it first takes food into its mouth, where it is mixed with saliva (which contains the first enzymes that kick-start the digestive process). It then passes via the gullet (the oesophagus) directly into the crop. The crop is a temporary food-storage area, and at the end of the day, a chicken's dinner will often show up as a bulge in the bird's chest, just above its breast and below its throat. It's in the crop that the food is softened up: mash and pellets are pretty soft already, so are broken down almost immediately, but grains and cereals are harder, and can take several hours to become soft.

The food then passes to a glandular stomach, the proventriculus, which acts as the 'pre-digester'; here, the food is mixed with digestive juices, pepsin and hydrochloric acid. Next, the food is passed into the gizzard – a small, circular organ, with flat sides and ribbed muscles – where it is milled, or ground down, by muscle action and sharp grit so that the food can pass into the duodenum and large intestine. On its journey to the intestines, the food receives juices from the pancreas and liver: the bile from the pancreas neutralises the acids from the stomach and works to break down the larger fat molecules, while enzymes from the liver set to work on the proteins, sugars and smaller fat molecules. Once digested, the nutrients are absorbed through the walls of the small intestine, and once past this part, water is reabsorbed into the body in the large intestine.

Undigested material passes to the cloaca, where it is mixed with urinary waste products; from the cloaca, this waste is expelled through the vent. Note that chickens don't urinate like other animals because birds don't have bladders. The kidneys do the work of removing the waste in the form of a thick, white substance known as urates, and this is expelled through the vent when the chicken passes a dropping. You'll spot the white-coloured urates easily: it surrounds the darker-coloured faeces formed from undigested food. Chickens will defecate between twenty-five and fifty times a day (and up to 50 per cent of their faeces passes out of the bird's body during the night).

Inspecting their droppings is an important way of determining the health of your birds: remember that a healthy bird's normal droppings are greenish-brown, with a little white in it, while the texture is quite firm and dry; wet, slimy faeces are an indication of diarrhoea (for treatment of this, see Chapter 9, page 219).

A balanced diet: mash and pellets

Whether organic or not, poultry feeds that are available in different forms to suit different ages and types of birds all contain a carefully controlled and formulated mixture of vital ingredients: protein, fats, calcium, vitamins and trace elements. Most are available in the form of either mash or pellets suitable for laying hens, chicks, young, growing birds and breeding birds, as well as for any birds that you want to fatten for the table.

Poultry, or laying, mash – which is sometimes also called layers' meal – contains the same nutrients as pellets, the only difference being that the mash has not been compressed and formed into pellet shapes and can be ground into different degrees of coarseness. The process of consuming mash and of eating pellets differs, however: eating mash is,

for chickens, like us having to eat with a knife and fork, when we have to eat politely and slowly; eating pellets is a bit like us eating with our hands, when we tend to rush and gobble our food.

Mash, which is a mixture of ground-up grains and added nutrients, can be given to chickens dry, which means that the birds have to work a bit harder when they eat it rather than simply gobbling it down, which also means that they don't grow quite as fat so quickly. The disadvantage of this is that dry mash tends to be scattered about as the birds rummage around their feeding stations, so prevent too much wastage by filling your chickens' bowls only half-full of mash and by using feeding bowls with inward-turning rims. Mash can also be mixed with a little water to form the consistency of a crumbly meal, which is often a favourite with the more greedy birds. The problem with wet mash, though, is that any leftovers must be removed from the coop after a few hours because it quickly goes off.

Spillage, and the consequent waste of dry mash, is why many poultry-keepers prefer to buy chicken pellets (also called layers' pellets). These are made from the same ingredients as mash, but are instead steamed and pressed through a metal sheet perforated with holes of different sizes to create 'strings' that are then broken to form pellets (or are further ground down to produce crumbs for chicks). Compared to mash, these compressed pellets don't allow the chickens to pick out their favourite, tasty bits and leave the rest behind, so they consequently eat all of the pellets and swallow all of the nutrients that they contain. Note that pellets are also favoured over mash for bearded and crested birds because mash can stick to their feathers, and food stuck to topknots not only spoils feathers, but must also appear to other birds rather like a waiter bearing a tray of canapés looks to party guests, the result being that the other chickens just can't resist having a little peck at the passing food stuck to the bird's head, which can, of course, cause injury.

If you do feed your chickens compressed pellets, make sure that they are the right size for your birds: standard layers' pellets will be too big for small bantams, for instance. Manufacturers have taken the sizes of breeds into account in their food preparation, and you will find some that will suit your birds among the different-sized compressed pellets available.

Food for all: feed composition

Like all animals, including humans, growing chickens need a different diet to that required by adult birds. Hens that are laying eggs for consumption also require a completely different diet to those that are laying a clutch of eggs to be hatched into chicks. The hatching egg contains a chicken to be, so the mother hen must be fed in such a way that her egg provides the optimal nutritional environment for the chick developing inside. That said, broody hens eat very little when actually sitting on their eggs, so care over their diet must be taken in advance. When brooding, hens require little more than a simple diet of mixed corn with plenty of maize to maintain their body mass and heat, as well as plenty of fresh drinking water.

FEED FOR CHICKS

Just before a chick hatches from its egg, it consumes what's left of the yolk, and this provides the infant bird with enough energy to tide it over during the first two days of its life. After this, chicks must be encouraged to eat and drink: they need the right level of protein or they will become severely malnourished and may die. The mother hen will usually lead by example, and will teach her chicks to eat, but you may sometimes have to step in to help. If so, a little mashed hard-boiled egg, or a little finely chopped spring onion added to the chick-crumb feed, will encourage them to eat, and you can teach them to drink by holding them gently and dipping their beaks into the water – they'll soon learn what it is. While a chick can survive if it loses half of its body weight, losing just one-tenth of its body's moisture content will lead to its death, which is why it's vital that you not only provide your chicks with constantly available fresh water, but that they are able to access it: this means that the drinker must be positioned at a chicken-friendly height and that the water should not be so deep that they could drown in it. They must also be encouraged to drink.

Chicks are typically fed on a proprietary chick feed – chick mash or chick pellets – known as chick starter feed, which is both nutritionally balanced, and, most importantly, the right size for tiny beaks. As an extra, they may have a little chick crumb, which is a mixture of various broken-up (to make them small) seeds and grains. In all cases, look for, and purchase, chick feed marked with the letters 'ACS': this stands for anti-coccidiostat, and it indicates that the feed contains an additive designed to protect chicks against the disease coccidiosis.

In most cases, this 'small feed' can be gradually phased out after about six weeks, when the chickens can be switched to growers' pellets or mash, but some inbred strains and more true bantams may need to remain on chick feed until they are around eight weeks old because their bodies are less efficient when it comes to absorbing all of the nutrients in their food.

TOP: The mother hen will teach her chicks by example, but you may need to help a little.

BOTTOM: As chicks grow, they can be introduced to regular chicken feed.

feeding chickens 115

FEED FOR YOUNG, GROWING BIRDS

Young birds are fed growers' rations: this is feed that is lower in protein and vitamins than chick feed. Pullets – hens aged from eight to twenty weeks old – shouldn't be overfed or given too much protein lest they grow too quickly while still internally immature. This could cause egg-laying problems later, and possibly also a partial moult when the hens are at POL (point-of-lay).

If your new birds are still quite young, they will probably still be being fed with growers' pellets or mash. When the hens are about eighteen weeks old, the feed should gradually be switched to layers' mash or pellets, which is a different mix devised to encourage egg production. So if your birds are still on growers' mash at this age, they need gradually to be weaned on to layers' mash, and you can do this by simply increasing the amount of layers' mash that you give them over a period of about a week to ten days. The same principle applies if you want to switch the feed from mash to pellets (or vice versa): suddenly presenting chickens with a completely new feed can be quite confusing for them, and they may not even recognise it as food.

FEED FOR LAYING HENS

Most, although by no means all, domestic chicken-keepers keep hens for laying eggs. These hens need a diet that is suited to egg production, and one that provides them with all of the nutrients that they need for a healthy life. Layers' mash and layers' pellets are complete feeds, but before buying any, check the label carefully because it should contain 16–17 per cent protein, as well as the extra calcium needed for shell production; additionally, the label should state that fibre and vitamins are in the mix.

Vitamins A and D are especially important vitamins for laying hens. Vitamin D is made within the body in response to sunlight; free-ranging birds living in a sunny climate will therefore probably derive sufficient vitamin D from wandering around outside each day, but in more temperate zones, and during the short days of the long, winter months, a feed to which this vitamin has been added will be necessary because it's vital for the absorption of calcium and phosphorous, which are required to create strong bones and good shells. Vitamin A helps chickens develop and maintain strong, healthy skin and healthy digestive and respiratory tracts and reproductive organs, and yellow maize, as well as all green- and yellow-coloured vegetables, contain high levels of this vitamin. When checking the list of ingredients, also look for trace minerals, such as selenium, which is needed to maintain health; methionine, an essential amino acid that assists in the breaking-down of fat and that keeps the digestive and 'urinary' system healthy; and copper sulphate, which is needed by chickens to convert feed into energy.

FEED FOR BREEDING BIRDS

Just as a growing bird needs different food to one who is laying eggs for consumption, so chickens that are laying clutches to be hatched require a feed whose composition comprises a special mix of nutrients. Breeding birds need a plentiful supply of protein, trace minerals and vitamins in their feed to ensure that their offspring are strong and healthy. And breeders' rations, as the name suggests, is what these birds are usually fed; it's also suited to birds from which you are intending to breed next year's stock, who can therefore be fed breeders' rations from mid-winter onwards.

FEED FOR BROODY HENS

When a broody hen is sitting on her clutch of eggs, she will eat very little, and requires nothing more than a simple diet of mixed corn with plenty of maize in order to maintain her weight and body temperature. She will also require plenty of fresh water, but note that because she is being fed on grain, her droppings will be quite dry, so she won't foul her clutch or nest.

feeding chickens **117**

FEED FOR TABLE BIRDS

Cockerels that are surplus to requirements are often kept by chicken-keepers and raised to provide meat for the table. Such birds can be fed household scraps in addition to a high-protein, fattening meal that will bulk them up. Not only will the birds gain weight as a result, they will also produce more flavoursome meat for the table because a varied diet – especially one that includes maize – makes these birds' flesh 'self-basting'. To see whether a (live) cockerel is oven-ready, pick him up, 'guestimate' his weight and feel his breast, which should be nice and firm. Cockerels as young as ten weeks of age may be ready for the table, and these young birds are known as poussins in the catering trade.

Feeding during the moult

Birds start to moult their feathers in late summer, shedding the old ones and growing new ones. As well as looking a bit the worse for wear, hens will also stop laying at this time. Don't cut back on their feed, though, because they will need to be well fed and well nourished (note that their diet should include plenty of protein) so that they grow new feathers, a process that can take up to three months to complete.

Ex-battery hens: food and drink

The annual moult and accompanying non-laying period is the main reason why battery hens are culled in commercial situations: no commercial producer wants the expense of feeding full rations to non-productive birds for an extended period. Rescuing battery hens from this fate and then bringing them on can be extremely rewarding, and not just for animal-welfare reasons, but also because the small-scale chicken-keeper can restore these birds to full egg-laying capacity, with many happily continuing to lay for many years to come.

Former battery hens will most likely have been fed on layers' mash, so will be used to this, but check at the rescue or rehoming centre from which you're obtaining them to be sure. (And note that in Britain, the leading organisation dedicated to the rescue and rehoming of battery hens is the Battery Hen Welfare Trust, which is based in Devon.) One important consideration to bear in mind about rescued battery hens is that they will have been used to 'nipple drinkers', which measured out their drinking water one drop at a time, so they will need to be shown that they can drink from a water bowl when you get them home.

Quality counts

Whatever breed or size of chickens you keep, and whether you keep them for laying, breeding or showing, give them the best-quality food. Buy your feed from a reputable supplier and make sure that it is clearly labelled with both the contents and the sell-by date. Don't buy food that is old or past its prime in order to save money: it could be dusty, mouldy, contaminated with rat or mouse urine or just the wrong food for your chickens' needs, and it could cause serious illness or even death. And if you tip the feed into a bucket and dust flies everywhere, take it back to your supplier and demand a refund. All in all, buy the best-quality layers' mash or pellets and grain feed, and your chickens will be the better for it.

Quantities

Exactly how much feed chickens should be given depends on their breed size, how much exercise they get, whether they are brooding or laying, and – just like us humans – on how warm or chilly the weather is. In winter, chickens need more food than they do in summer, in order to keep warm. Very young chicks will need feeding four or five times a day, until they are reasonably active and strong enough to feed themselves from a small trough or hopper designed for 'on demand' eating. On average, an adult chicken will eat between 100 and 125 g (3½–4 oz) of feed every day, which includes their allowance of grain (see below, pages 124 to 126). Large breeds may require more: up to 150 g (6 oz) daily.

You will have to observe your birds carefully to determine the correct quantities. Give your chickens their breakfast and then, after one hour, check to see whether there is any food left. If there is none left, gradually increase the amount of food on offer until there is no food left by noon. Conversely, if there is food left at midday, decrease the amount that you are giving your birds at breakfast. If the birds are free-ranging, don't be tempted to overfeed them, and remember that it's better to give these birds their feed in the late afternoon or towards evening, and in their pen or roost, because that way, you are attracting them back home, to safety.

Storing feed

Just as you keep your own food in hygienic conditions, so, too, should you store your chicken feed carefully and safely. Keep it in a cool, dry, well-ventilated place that is protected from vermin, wild birds, dust, dirt and your household pets. Also remember to check and keep a record of your chicken feed's sell-by/use-by date, and never give chickens food that has passed its expiry date. It may have been contaminated for a start, while the beneficial vitamins and medications with which it has been formulated will be less effective, at best, and totally ineffective, at worst.

Don't let a feed bag rest directly on a stone, tile or concrete floor because no matter how dry it appears to be, condensation will form at the base of the bag; instead, place it on a pallet. A large rubbish bin or dustbin made of galvanised metal is a better storage container than a plastic one because rodents can't chew through metal so easily. So a metal container with a tight, securely fitting lid is ideal for feed. Store it in a shed or outhouse, in which you can also set out baited traps or poison for rats and mice (that is, as long as household cats or dogs have no access to it).

If you are storing relatively small amounts of feed, also try to keep it in a galvanised-metal container with a tight-fitting lid. Don't use glass storage jars because their contents could be mistaken for human food, and clear glass also allows sunlight to penetrate the jar, destroying the feed's vitamin content.

Additives and supplements

Chickens that are fed good-quality feed – and a feed that is right for their age and purpose – along with plenty of fresh greens, should not need any additional vitamins or minerals because their feed is formulated to provide them with all of the vital nutrients that they require. Just like humans, though, there are times when an additional nutritional boost can help: during the moult, for instance, or when rearing birds or during the dark, cold, winter months (especially if your birds don't have access to fresh grass).

Soluble vitamins (available from veterinary surgeries) can be placed in the birds' drinking water (see left) and used for about five days. A more natural supplement is apple-cider vinegar (ACV), which has

been used for centuries as a pick-me-up for both humans and livestock. Many chicken-keepers maintain that ACV is a great tonic, especially for stressed birds and during the moult, when their energy levels may be a little low. It can be diluted with water and given to your chickens in a water dish (and it's not surprising that chickens will drink it because they love apples). Make sure, however, that any ACV you buy is unfiltered – you may have to go to a whole-food, organic or health-food store to find it – and not the clear product that you see on supermarket shelves.

Mixed-grain feed

Chickens' main meals of mash or pellets already contain grains in their composition, as well as all of the vitamins and minerals that they need. However, in addition to the ground-up grains in these, but as part of their daily allowance of food, chickens can be given a mixed-grain feed: 20 g (¾ oz) of grain per day for a laying hen is about right in summer (free-ranging birds who are grubbing about for natural titbits won't require so much), while in winter you could increase the ration to 25–30 g (around 1 oz). All chickens love grain mixes, but because their cereals and grains are hard to digest, they are best given on their own as the afternoon or early evening feed that ensures that the birds go to bed on a full crop. Don't give your chickens a combined meal of mash (or pellets) and grain: this would be completely useless because they would eat only the grain first, would then become full up, and would consequently ignore their mash (or pellets). A broody hen – if she is eating at all – can enjoy an exclusively mixed-grain diet if you want her to hatch the eggs, a bonus being that her droppings will also become drier, so that the eggs don't become fouled.

...CHING FOR SCATTERED GRAIN GRAIN KEEPS CHICK-
...MINDS AND BODIES ACTIVE.

Scattering the grain around to make your birds search and work for it keeps their brains occupied and their bodies exercised. Giving your chickens grain is a useful way of encouraging new birds to get to know you, and once they know that you have some, they will soon be happy to eat it from the palm of your hand. When shaken in a bucket or container, the grains also make a distinctive rattling noise with which you can summon your flock at supper and bedtime – they'll soon learn what the sound promises, and will come racing home!

Mixed-grain feed usually contains wheat, oats, corn and sometimes sunflower seeds. Note that this mix is given to birds in addition to their main food of mash or pellet feed, and that it should not be fed to them as their main diet. If chickens don't get enough exercise – perhaps because they are confined to a run – they can easily become fat if they are given too much grain. And if they are young, growing birds, they can put on weight very fast – too fast for their immature internal organs, so that if fat is deposited around a hen's ovaries, for instance, these may be damaged and her egg-laying ability impaired. Cocks' fertility can also be adversely affected if they are overweight, not to mention the discomfort that a hen has to endure when a hefty cock is balancing on her back (that's if he is able to get 'in the mood' at all!) In addition, too much grain can cause obesity in mature chickens and, just as in all animals – humans included – being obese puts undue strain on the heart, lungs and legs.

Note that small breeds have proportionately small beaks and can't always manage whole grains; broken grains are smaller, and there are also mixed grains for bantams that are suited to their size. Another consideration when it comes to commercially prepared grain mixes is that they often contain barley, and in the experience of many chicken-keepers, chickens and bantams dislike this, so will often pick out the grains that they prefer and will leave the barley behind. And when birds do eat the barley, it

feeding chickens **125**

can furthermore make them fat, and overweight hens are not productive layers. The inclusion of this bulking agent is therefore annoying: it adds to the cost of the feed, but is generally wasted, so read a feed's label carefully if you want to avoid buying it.

Alternatively, you could make your own mix of wheat and maize, whose ratio must not be more than 1 part maize to 3 parts wheat (although you could add a little more maize in winter to help your chickens maintain their body heat). To this basic grain mix, you could then add ground oats, sunflower seeds (but not salted ones), linseeds and bran. Sprouted seeds and grains are also a great addition – and a good source of vitamins in winter – and try oats (or alfalfa, which you can sprinkle on your own salads too!) (Note that you will first need to soak the seeds or grains overnight in a jar or bucket of water; drain off the liquid the next day, place the container in a warm place and then stir or shake the seeds or grains up to three times a day; they'll sprout quickly, and will add nutrition and variety to your chickens' diets.) Add the spouted seeds when the green tops have grown to about 1 cm (½ in) long. Additionally, a few sultanas tossed into the mix make for tasty treats.

While maize improves the colour of egg yolks, and often also the legs of yellow-legged breeds intended for showing, remember that it's important to keep to the 25:75 ratio because too much maize in a laying hen's diet can cause fat to be deposited around her ovaries. And maize fed to birds that are being reared for the table will give their flesh that distinctive, yellow, 'corn-fed' colour. But above all, bear in mind that mixed-grain feed should be provided as part of your chickens' overall daily feed allowance, and not in addition to, or as a replacement for, their main feeds of mash or pellets.

Grit: the vital ingredient

Feeding your birds plenty of the right food is only part of the feeding process, because without grit in their diet, they won't be able to digest any of it! Earlier, in the information given on chickens' digestive systems (see pages 109 to 110), I observed that chickens don't have teeth with which to chew, and instead rely on muscle action and the addition of little 'millstones' of grit in the gizzard with which to break down food for digestion. There is a variety of types of grit sold for chickens, all of which should be available from your feed-supplier, so make sure that you have this to hand alongside their feed. Indeed, ensure that you always have a ready supply of grit for your chickens, and a small container of grit placed in the henhouse or run will be ideal for them to access.

Mixed grit consists of burnt and ground-down oyster shells. This is calcium-rich – and very much required by laying hens in order to form strong eggshells – and also contains many beneficial trace minerals. Many chicken-keepers don't give mixed grit to their hens because they are feeding their birds the best-quality layers' mash or pellets, which already contains plenty of calcium. However, others provide a thin layer of mixed grit in nest boxes; remember that laying an egg takes up to two hours, and that a hen will therefore be in her nesting box for some time, so that if it is present, she can peck away at the mixed grit if, and when, she feels that she needs it. But note that if you've got straw or hay in your nest boxes, then you must offer this grit in a separate bowl as it's quite fine and would otherwise get lost amid the straw or hay.

Granite grit is the most vital grit for chickens, who require it for their digestion. This consists of tiny stones that are sharper than the ground oyster shells in mixed grit, and that go to work breaking down food within a chicken's gizzard. You can provide your chickens with granite grit in a separate bowl or else mix it up with some mixed grit, but then it's a good idea to put some fine charcoal through the mix to aid digestion.

Even if your chickens run free, you should always provide them with a dish of mixed grit and granite grit because these are not always present in sufficient quantities in every garden, while any fine stones found in the garden often have smooth edges that don't grind down chicken feed as efficiently as granite-grit stones.

Free-ranging chickens

While free-range chickens can feed for themselves, you need to make sure there is nothing dangerous they could eat. Chickens that are allowed to roam free will usually have access to a plentiful supply of green stuff, and be warned that unless you fence off your vegetable plot or flowerbeds, your birds will happily scratch these up and will eat everything in sight. Free-ranging chickens are, however, highly effective weeders: they'll feast on the leaves and shoots of perennial and annual weeds, so there's less work for you to do. And because they are omnivorous, they will also eat insects, snails (their favourites) and the odd slug. So when digging over your vegetable beds during the autumn and winter, encourage your birds to earn their keep: let them scratch up the turned-over soil, and they'll eat the grubs of any pests lurking there, reducing your need for pesticides. But don't give them any hairy caterpillars because their hairs can irritate chickens' throats (and left on their own, chickens will probably have a good look at a hairy caterpillar and will then walk away from it).

Although they are unlikely to eat them anyway, chickens who roam free (or any other chickens, for that matter) should not be fed any of the following plants that may be found in gardens or in wild or rural locations, either as fresh greens or in scraps, as they can be toxic to birds.

• Aconite (also known as monkshood, blue rocket and wolfsbane). Although aconite is very pretty, this hardy perennial plant is also poisonous to humans.
• Bryony (also known as English mandrake). Bryony is poisonous to humans, as well as to chickens.
• Dock seeds. If you have nettles on your land, then growing beside them will be dock plants. Dock leaves are harmless, but the seeds must be avoided by chickens.
• Groundsel, which is a very common weed in vegetable gardens, especially where the soil has been newly turned for cultivation. If your chickens are scratching around the vegetable plot, they shouldn't eat groundsel anyway, but make sure that you don't pull it up and add it to their greens.
• Horseradish. Cultivated for its root for culinary use, the leaves of this plant are toxic to chickens, so if you are growing it, fence off this crop to keep the chickens away.
• Hemlock. Also known as 'mother die', hemlock was the principle ingredient in the 'poison cups' used by the ancient Athenians as a method of execution: among its most famous victims were Thermanes, Phocion and Socrates. Hemlock grows wild across all of the temperate zones in weedy, moist and warm spots by the edges of fields and streams. All parts of the plant, and especially the seeds, are highly poisonous to chickens and humans.

• Henbane. Once one of the 'magic ingredients' of a witches' brew, henbane grows across Europe and Eurasia, later having been introduced to North America, Australia and Brazil. It is most often found growing on waste ground and roadsides.

• Laburnum. Laburnum is a very attractive ornamental tree, whose pretty pods of seeds are toxic to both chickens and humans.

• Privet. Although they'll happily sit, shelter or nest underneath a plant that, more often than not, forms garden hedges, chickens won't eat privet. It's toxic, so don't add any hedge trimmings to their greens.

• Rhubarb. The leaves of the rhubarb 'fruit' are toxic, to chickens and humans.

• Thistles. Chickens won't eat thistles because they're too tough and too bristly, which is just as well, as they would poison the birds.

Because many of these plants may find their way on to them, chickens should not be allowed to roam around and peck on compost heaps – as tempting as it may be – in case they accidentally ingest a plant that is dangerous. So keep compost heaps fenced off from chickens.

In addition, chickens must never be given the following:

• eggshells (because this could encourage egg-eating behaviour);

• potato leaves or raw potatoes (although cooked potatoes and the boiled skins of potatoes are alright);

• tomato leaves (tomatoes and potatoes are members of the nightshade family).

Never give chickens any leftover animal protein, be it fish, meat or fowl. And although they will eat grubs and insects, chickens must not be fed any meat products in order to prevent their possible infection with salmonella, which could be introduced from meat products.

the chicken keeper's handbook

Leftovers and treats

In addition to their mash or pellet rations, all chickens – whether free-roaming or confined to folds and runs – should have access to a daily supply of fresh green vegetables: grass, spinach, lettuce, kale, cabbage, sprouts, cauliflower leaves and broccoli stalks, for example. Put them in a manger-type feeder a little off the ground so that the chickens have to stretch to get them, thereby providing the birds with a bit of work to keep them occupied and a little extra exercise to keep them fit. You could also give them grated or slighted cooked (just softened) carrots, turnips or Swedes, which you could either mix with their mash or serve separately, as a 'side dish'! Ideally, each chicken should receive about 29 g (1 oz) of fresh greens a day, which is not a great amount, but enough to keep them satisfied and healthy. Don't give them any more, though, because they won't otherwise eat their rations, which have been designed to keep them in tiptop condition.

On cold days, potato skins boiled in unsalted water, mixed, when slightly warm, with layers' mash makes a very welcome and sustaining treat, as do leftover pasta and rice (but not curry, otherwise the chickens' eggs will taste equally spicy!) Porridge also seems to go down well in winter – for a while, at least, because chickens seem to get bored with it. Toast crusts or bread cut into cubes can be scattered on the ground, or soaked in water to make a soggy mess; chickens find this quite delicious, but even more tasty is bread and butter (or margarine). Chickens also like fruit, especially apples (this is one way to get rid of windfalls and bruised fruit) and blackberries, while even an orange will be gobbled up by them, providing them with vitamin C.

FRESH GREEN VEGETABLES ARE ANN ESSENTIAL - AND TASTY
- PART OF A CHICKEN'S DIET.

CHAPTER SEVEN

Which breeds?

There are more than a hundred different breeds of chickens to choose from, including established pure breeds (which are further categorised as light breeds, heavy breeds, true bantams and game breeds), and each has its own distinctive colour, plumage, size and behavioural characteristics. Many small-scale and domestic chicken-keepers keep such breeds both for pleasure and for their eggs, their meat, for breeding and for showing. In addition to the pure breeds, there are also hybrid chickens, and if you are interested in keeping only a few hens for egg production, then these birds are ideal.

Hybrids: eggs galore!

A hybrid chicken is the result of a cross between two or more breeds. At the end of World War I, when the demand for fresh eggs increased significantly, commercial poultry-keepers began selective-breeding programmes using such breeds as the Rhode Island Red, White Leghorn and Light Sussex (which were known as high performers), so creating the first hybrid chickens. There are two types of hybrids: the egg-producers, and the meat, or table, birds (known as broilers). And since the end of World War II, these birds have formed the backbone of the poultry industry.

HYBRID LAYERS

Hybrid layers are usually a good deal cheaper to buy than pure-breed hens, and are normally supplied already vaccinated against the most serious poultry diseases. Because they are prolific egg-layers, these hybrids make an excellent choice for the smallholder, or the backyard hen-keeper who has limited space, but wants a ready supply of fresh eggs. Robust and resilient, these hybrid layers are also ideal for the novice poultry-keeper (and children), who still need to gain experience in poultry-keeping.

Although the range of hybrid 'breeds' is not as great as that of the pure breeds, it is growing in number. Those that are based on the Rhode Island Red will lay light-brown-coloured eggs. But if you prefer white-shelled eggs, then Leghorn-based hybrids are the chickens for you. And if you want something a little more exotic, then try the Fenton Blue, a hybrid layer that produces a variety of tinted eggs that range in colour from olive-green to pale blue.

HYBRID BROILERS: TABLE BIRDS

Modern hybrid broilers are, for the most part, crosses of White Rock and Cornish Game birds, a combination that has produced table birds with a high meat-to-bone ratio, which grow rapidly, and to a significant size. Many people, however, feel that the taste of their meat is not as tasty as that of pure-breed birds.

Hybrid broilers can be easily kept by the domestic poultry-keeper, partly because they do not require elaborate fencing in: they're too big and heavy to fly, or, indeed, to move very far! Furthermore, they are quite gentle in nature, and their placid temperament therefore makes them ideal pets or companion birds for both humans and other chickens. The main problem with hybrid broilers is that they tend to become overweight, which can put undue stress on the heart and also can cause leg problems and deformities. Today, breeders are introducing newer hybrids that have a slightly slower growth rate, and when these broilers are allowed to range free and/or are given a lower-protein feed, their weight problems diminish greatly.

Dual-purpose breeds

Many of the heavy breeds of poultry (see below, pages 154 to 166) were originally kept to provide eggs and meat: the surplus cockerels were fattened up for the table, while at the end of their productive life, the pullets kept for eggs were also killed and eaten. Like hybrids, such dual-purpose breeds are a good choice for the novice poultry-keeper as they are docile and can be easily handled, not being as flighty as many other breeds (which means that high fences aren't required to contain them). They are very good-looking birds, too.

Dual-purpose pure breeds of chickens can also be shown at poultry exhibitions, which is both fun and informative because such shows are a great way of finding out about new developments, products and concerns in poultry-keeping and breeding. But just like their canine equivalents, the standards for entry to poultry shows require you have some knowledge of breed standards – the plumage colour, comb type and shape, feather type and overall weight, for instance, must all be perfect – and just like dogs, chickens need to be groomed and trained in order to show themselves at their finest.

Show types

At shows, birds are categorised according to types, notably hard feather, soft feather, light breeds, heavy breeds, bantams, true bantams and rare breeds.

HARD-FEATHER BREEDS

Hard-feather breeds have short, tight feathering that follows the shape of the body closely, and the term is applied to game birds that were historically used for cock-fighting. In appearance, these game birds generally have an upright, challenging station (carriage), with hard, highly developed muscles and, in some instances, a featherless breastbone (so that the opponents of fighting birds have less to get a grip on).

The Old English Game and the Malay and Indian Game are typical examples of hard-feathered birds. Many of these birds are specialist and show-ring breeds. Not only are they not noted for their egg production, but they are also often noisy birds, and sometimes quite aggressive to both humans and other birds.

SOFT-FEATHER BREEDS

'Soft-feather breeds' is the term used for all breeds that are not hard-feathered, which means that it's possible to have soft-feathered heavy breeds and soft-feathered light breeds, the key identifying feature of these soft-feathered breeds being, as their name implies, a loose and fluffy feathering that often disguises the bird's body shape.

In some breeds, the feathering is quite striking: the aptly named Frizzle, which was developed purely for exhibiting, has curly feathers, for instance; the Poland is noted for its fantastic pompom-like head feathers (and is available in Frizzle form, too); while the Silkie looks like a ball of fluff topped by a powder puff. These birds are favourites in the show ring, and require special care and attention in order to maintain their unusual plumage.

LIGHT AND HEAVY BREEDS

Light chicken breeds generally originated in the Mediterranean region, and are best known for their egg-laying capacity, and for producing white-shelled eggs. Light breeds are not favoured as broilers (table or meat birds) and can be flighty, excitable and nervous in character. Typical examples of light breeds are the Leghorn and the Ancona; see also below, pages 146 to 154.

Heavy breeds are birds that were developed for their utility, that is, they are good for the table and are pretty good egg-layers, too. These birds tend to be large and docile and are ideally suited to the domestic environment, making them ideal 'first birds' for the novice poultry-keeper. Examples of heavy-breed chickens are the Orpington, the Rhode Island Red and the Sussex; see also below, pages 154 to 166.

FRIZZLE BANTAM

BANTAMS AND TRUE BANTAMS

If space is limited, bantams are a good choice for the poultry-keeper. Note that there are important differences between true bantams and bantams.

True bantams (see also below, pages 144 to 146) are naturally small birds and breeds in their own right, but most true bantams don't have any utility role – they are not prolific eggs-layers, and their small size makes them less useful as table birds – which means that in many instances, they are kept purely for their gorgeous good looks and for exhibition purposes.

Bantams, on the other hand, are miniaturised versions of conventionally sized chicken breeds, just as dwarf plants or trees are mini-versions of the bigger, parent species. Today, there are bantam versions of nearly all of the most popular chicken breeds. Apart from being smaller, they are otherwise identical to their larger relatives, and the breed regulations now generally specify that bantams should be half the weight of their 'big' equivalents.

RARE BREEDS

The term 'rare breed' doesn't necessarily mean that a particular breed of chicken is in imminent danger of dying out. Instead, it refers to breeds that don't have a specialist club or association to promote interest in them (and consequently their survival), but that are supported by a small number of enthusiastic poultry-keepers. In Britain, the interests of such rare breeds of chickens as the Norfolk Grey and the Vorwerk are looked after by the Rare Breeds Survival Trust and the Rare Poultry Society. See also below, pages 166 to 172.

A selection of breeds

The breeds that follow constitute just a small number of the possible choices for the domestic poultry-keeper. 'Specialist' breeds that require a high level of experience have been omitted in favour of those that are ideal for the beginner, while others are more suited to those with a little more experience. Some breeds are noted for their egg production; others, for their dual purpose or utility. And remember that many heavy and light breeds have smaller, bantam forms.

In addition to a description of the breed – its appearance, colour, plumage and so on – a note is made regarding its character – whether it is docile, excitable or noisy – as well as its utility value as an egg-producer or table bird. Understanding a little about the qualities of each breed will help you to choose the right breed for your needs and circumstances.

TRUE BANTAMS
True bantams are essentially very small breeds of chickens, and although these breeds are very ancient, many are highly adapted to modern living.

Booted Bantam
The Booted Bantam's name is the first indicator of its appearance: it has feathered legs that make it look as though it is wearing boots. The appearance of these 'boots' is created by long 'vulture hocks' formed by long, stiff quill feathers on the hock joint. The Booted Bantam's plumage colour and patterning range

NTAM ROOSTER.

from barred through black, buff, Columbian, millefleur, partridge, pearl grey and porcelain to white. A short, compact bird, with a broad back and wings held low, the cock has a red, well-serrated, five-point comb; the wattles and earlobes are likewise red.

A popular bird in continental Europe, this breed has been kept domestically since the seventeenth century in the Netherlands. Docile and friendly, Booted Bantams like to run free (but their 'boots' prevent them from scratching up the ground too much). In summer, they are good producers of quite tiny eggs that range from white to tinted in colour.

Dutch Bantam

A very easy breed to care for, the Dutch Bantam is one of the smallest – and friendliest – true bantam breeds, and encompasses more than twenty different varieties, including buff Columbian, lavender, salmon, silver duckwing, cuckoo, black, white and buff. Although they are small, Dutch Bantam hens are good layers (they produce up to 160 eggs a year, albeit small ones) and thrive in even quite limited spaces, making them ideal for eglus (see pages 78 to 79) and backyard hen-keeping. Upright in stature, and with a deep, 'U'-shaped back, the Dutch Bantam is also a very attractive bird, with plenty of ornamental feathers; a lovely, full, upright tail; white, almond-shaped earlobes; and legs that vary from a dark-blue to a light-blue slate colour. Dutch Bantams can be a little flighty, so you'll need to consider suitable ways of confining them.

Pekin

Docile, yet quite cheeky, the Pekin is a terrific bird if you are looking for a breed that is very attractive, friendly and full of personality, and that is a good egg-producer, too. With a short, broad body that looks as though it's tilting forwards, and short, feathered legs with masses of soft hackle feathers, the Pekin can resemble a lovely, soft ball of fluff. Its varieties of colours and patterns include barred, black, blue and buff, Columbian, cuckoo, mottled, lavender, partridge and white, making the Pekin a delight to see in the garden. Because of its small size, it is ideally suited to limited spaces, but – as with all 'feathered-foot' varieties – note that extra care must be taken to ensure that these are kept clean and dry.

LIGHT BREEDS
Here is a selection of some of the breeds that are classified as light breeds.

Derbyshire Redcap

Sometimes known simply as the 'Redcap', the Derbyshire Redcap is closely associated with the English county of Derbyshire, where it originated as a dual-purpose bird. Today, many of its enthusiastic supporters value it for its relative rarity and for the numerous white eggs that the hens lay. Robust and long-lived, Redcaps enjoy foraging, so are best kept where they can roam free. As well as being good egg-layers, the hens are 'non-sitters'– that is, they don't go broody.

The hens are the most gorgeous nut-brown colour, with lovely spangling, while the males have orange-coloured hackles and saddles; both sexes have a black tail. The large comb – the males will take three years to develop fully their 'red cap'– is like a rose in shape, with spikes of an even height, and the members of this breed should always have red earlobes. (Note that the comb needs special protection in very cold winters, when a smear of petroleum jelly will help to prevent frostbite.)

Leghorn

The Leghorn is a well-known breed (thanks, no doubt, to the cartoon character who went by the name of 'Foghorn Leghorn') that originated in Livorno, in Italy (Leghorn is, in fact, the German name for the city). The breed's development took place in many other countries, however, particularly in the USA after 1835, when a consignment of Brown Leghorns was imported into New York by N P Ward and American breeders then set about encouraging the breed's egg-laying capacity. The fortunes of the town of Petaluma in California were almost entirely based on the Leghorn, and in 1916, the town held its first Annual Egg Day to celebrate this. By the time that the first White Leghorn arrived in Britain in 1879, the breed was already highly regarded as one of the best egg-producers around.

The American and British Leghorn breeds parted company in terms of their appearance many years ago. The American version maintains an appearance that is more related to the productive utility strains that were found before World War I, with a large tail and medium-sized comb, while the British version has a much shorter tail and a very large comb. (Breed standards in each country also recognise different colours.) What all Leghorns share, however, is the capacity to lay numerous white eggs, with the hens rarely going broody. As with all light breeds, Leghorns have a tendency to be a bit flighty, but are also active and very intelligent birds that enjoy human contact. They are ideal for the larger garden or run.

WHITE LEGHORN

Minorca

The Minorca (left) has a similar appearance to the Leghorn, and, like that breed, also originated in the Mediterranean, where the British spent several years during the eighteenth century fighting to gain control of the Balearic Islands. Although it is believed that the first examples of the breed were taken by the British from Minorca at this time, it's not until 1834 that we have the first documented evidence of the breed. Ironically, the Minorca is now almost extinct on the island that gave it its name, but enthusiasts throughout Spain and the rest of Europe have done much to generate interest in, and revive, the breed, and during the nineteenth century, a bantam-sized Minorca was developed that proved to be as prolific a layer as its full-sized relative.

The breed may be black, blue, white and buff, but the really distinctive feature of the Minorca is its enormous, oval-shaped, white-coloured earlobes. The cock's comb – which is large and single – is carried erect, while the hen's comb folds over. Less flighty than other light breeds, the rather bossy Minorca hens produce large, white eggs. Apart from taking care that their earlobes are not damaged, the very pretty Minorcas need no special attention and are a very good option for the novice poultry-keeper.

Scots Dumpy

Scottish in origin, and with very short legs, the Scots Dumpy (or Dumpie) is an ancient breed. It may well have been brought to Britain by the Romans, although the earliest record of the

breed in Scotland dates from the eighteenth century, and it was not until 1852 that it was first seen in England. The breed's short legs and rather heavy body are said to have developed because these birds were once kept on crofts and smallholdings that were surrounded by rough, open land, with plenty of predators, so they were bred this way to encourage them not to roam too far. Their physiognomy gives the birds a sort of waddling gait, which has led to them being given a number of nicknames over the years, such as creepers, crawlers and bakies.

The body of an adult Scots Dumpy is usually carried around 5 cm (2 in) above the ground, and it has a full tail, with well-arched sickle feathers. The head features a strong, curved beak, large, red eyes and a single serrated comb, while the neck is covered in quite long and flowing hackle feathers. Attractive birds, Scots Dumpies are reliable layers of cream-coloured eggs and make good

table birds, too. They have rather nice personalities as well, being reasonably docile, and make good backyard chickens for those with a little poultry-keeping experience. Note that breeding can be difficult, though, as the Scots Dumpy tends to revert to a longer-legged form, while crossing short-legged versions can lead to infertility and increased mortality rates. Nevertheless, the hens make terrific mothers, although they dislike being moved once they have made up their minds where they are going to sit.

Scots Grey

Proud, but a bit excitable, and elegant, yet very robust, the Scots Grey used to be known as the Scotch Grey (and colloquially as the Chick Marley). A pretty ancient breed, it's been a feature of many Scottish farms and homesteads for several centuries, having been developed as a farmyard fowl. A dual-purpose breed – although its egg

numbers aren't particularly high – it is happy to range free (bantam-sized Scots Grey prefer to roam freely, too), but is also temperamentally suited to being enclosed in runs. That said, the Scots Grey is a good forager that is not best suited to confinement because limited space makes these birds nervous and prone to feather-pecking, so if you have the space to let them roam around at will, the Scots Grey is a good choice.

Both the males and females are very good-looking birds, with large, amber-coloured eyes and bright-red combs, wattles and earlobes. These are full-breasted chickens that stand on strong, long, widely spaced legs, which are light in colour and featherless. The Scots Grey's gorgeous plumage displays a steel-grey-coloured ground, with distinctive black barring across all of the feathers. The males can be feisty – especially during the breeding season – but mature quite early (and their flesh is good for roasting), while happy, well-cared-for

hens will produce a fair number of good-sized, cream-coloured eggs. This is a beautiful breed that could do with being seen more widely outside Scotland.

Silkie

Hen 'history' indicates that the Silkie dates back to at least 1298, when the Venetian explorer Marco Polo described a chicken with 'hair like a cat' while on his travels to China. The breed is much older than that, too, and is very well documented in ancient Chinese literature as it was widely used in traditional medicine. (And more recent Western examination of the breed has revealed that Silkie meat contains a much higher proportion of carnosine – an important antioxidant – than that of other breeds.) The Silkie is therefore remarkable, on both the inside and the outside.

Although it is classified as a full-sized fowl, its naturally small stature – expect a large male to weigh no more than 1.8 kg (4 lb) – means that it's often mistaken for a bantam. (The tiny, 500 g/1 lb bantam-sized version of the breed was standardised in 1993.) Silkies have blue-black skin and dark flesh, too. The birds have five toes on each foot, feathered legs and turquoise-coloured earlobes and cushion combs. Because their feathers have no barbs to hold them together, as do other, 'normal' breeds, the Silkie does indeed have soft, fur-like plumage that grows in colours ranging from black through blue and gold to partridge and white. A disadvantage of their unique feathers is that they are not water-proof, unlike those of like other chickens, and must be kept dry and protected from bad weather.

Silkie hens' sole purpose in life appears to be motherhood; they are often crossbred with other species to make surrogate mothers and lay well in winter, frequently continuing when other breeds have stopped for the season. A Silkie hen will, on average, produce around a hundred creamy-brown-coloured eggs before she becomes broody.

Both male and female Silkies are gentle in nature, but don't mix well with other birds; they don't fly, and are happy to be kept in runs, as long as these are dry and mud-free. (Select their feeders and drinkers with care to make sure that their crests and beards avoid being soiled.) Silkies are good birds for beginners, but only if you are prepared to look after them well. Furthermore, note that some strains of this breed are prone to Marek's disease (see Chapter 9, page 216), so it's important to buy your Silkies from a reputable and experienced breeder, and to check that the birds have been fully vacci-nated.

Welsummer

For many poultry-keepers, the Welsummer (left) is the perfect-looking chicken: the standard colour for males is black-red and, for hens, partridge. Bred at the beginning of the twentieth century in the Ijssel valley, and taking its name from the village of Welsum, in the Netherlands, the Welsummer is the re-sult of crossbreeding Faverolles, Wyandottes, Brahmas, Cochins, Malays and Dorkings, with Barn-evelders being added into the mix to encourage a more uniform shape. Then, being keen to increase egg production, breeders introduced Rhode Island Reds and partridge-coloured Leghorns into the breeding programme, and the result was the alert and active Welsummer. Welsummer hens are famous for laying terracotta-coloured eggs (about 140 of them a year), and the hens that lay the fewest eggs lay the ones with the darkest colour. If you want dark eggs, then choose dark eggs for hatching and rearing, but if you want more eggs, raise chicks from lighter-coloured eggs! Welsummer hens are reluctant mothers, however, so if you want to hatch eggs, you'll need an incubator.

Great foragers, but equally suited to confinement, Welsummers are quite large birds for a light breed (a bantam version is also available), which is, perhaps, not surprising, given the numerous heavy breeds in their genetic mix. Child-friendly, docile Welsummers are additionally easy to handle, as well as being hardy, making them ideally suited to backyard life, as well as to the novice chicken-keeper.

HEAVY BREEDS

The following breeds are classified as heavy breeds.

Australorp

The name of the handsome Australorp breed is derived from a contraction of 'Australian Black Orpington', and the bird is the result of a cross between stock birds imported from Australia during the 1920s and the Black Orpington. Traditionally black in colour, with a magnificent, beetle-green sheen to the feathers when they catch the sunlight, white and blue-laced versions also appear. The medium-sized comb is single and serrated, and the eggs are tinted towards a pale-brown colour.

This breed is easy to keep: Australorps soon become very tame, and are happy to be handled (which means that they are great if you have children). They are not aggressive towards each other, so that even young cockerels that are kept as part of a breeding programme can be kept together without risk of displays of aggressive behaviour. Australorps don't mind being kept in runs, will adapt well to foraging and are quite hardy birds, too. They are also surprisingly economical eaters and mature early; note, though, that the hens can become a little hefty if they don't get plenty of exercise. The Australorp is a fine, dual-purpose bird, providing both eggs (about two hundred a year) and meat (which is white-skinned and very tasty).

THE BEAUTIFUL BLACK SHEEN OF THE AUSTRALORP.

Barnevelder

A comparatively new breed, the Barnevelder was exported from the Netherlands to the UK and North America during the 1920s. It takes its name from the small town of Barneveld, in the Dutch province of Gelderland, where it was developed by crossing local fowl with Asiatic breeds, including the Brahma, Langshan and Malay. The result was a good producer of large, dark-brown eggs (about 170 a year), which lighten in colour as a hen ages; a bird with a friendly character; and a gorgeous-looking chicken that's ideal for back-garden poultry-keeping. Robust and good-natured birds, Barnevelders are good foragers, but adapt well to confinement and also grow quickly.

In terms of its looks, the Barnevelder is characterised by a deep, broad and full body; a bright-red comb, wattles and earlobes; orange-brown eyes; and clean, yellow legs. Its plumage is very attractive, with dark hackle feathers, a beetle-green sheen and contrasting edging to the feathers. The breast is light brown, with brown and black lacing on the wings. In double-laced blue varieties, the black lacing is replaced by a light-blue colour, while black and white types are both solid-colour versions of the breed.

Brahma

Chickens don't come any bigger or more impressive than the Brahma (large males weigh up to 5.45 kg/12 lb, while large females can weigh up to 4.1 kg/9 lb), although bantam versions are available that are exact, albeit scaled-down, replicas of their larger relatives. This gorgeous, exotic-looking breed is believed to be the result of crosses between breeds imported into the USA from India (the Grey Chittagong) and China (the Shanghai), with a little Cochin possibly having been added to the mix, too. Its name certainly reflects the breed's origins: Brahma is a shortened form of Brahmaputra, one of the great Asiatic rivers that flows from China through India and Bangladesh before emptying into the Bay of Bengal. The Brahma was the breed that was sent to Queen Victoria in 1852 by the US breeder George Burnham, and the royal seal of approval soon made this bird very well known in Britain.

THE IMPRESSIVE BRAHMA

A BUFF BRAHMA BANTAM

Square and deep in body, with a short back, pro-fuse feathering and large, feathered legs, the cock is an especially striking bird. Regarding colours, there are buff Columbian, dark, gold, light and white varieties, and their fine appearance makes Brahmas very popular birds to keep. As to eggs, a productive young layer will lay around 140 small, light-brown eggs a year (the Brahma's egg-laying capacity was reduced as a result of the breeding of the bird for its plumage).

In spite of their size, male Brahmas are surpris-ingly timid, and may be bullied by cockerels of other breeds. The Brahma is also a breed that is slow to mature, taking around two years to be-come fully adult; these birds consequently tend to put on weight if they are overfed. Allowance must be made for their feathered legs, too – they must be kept in dry conditions – but the breed doesn't object to confinement, and the hens make good, broody mothers.

Cochin

The Cochin, an exotic, fully-feathered breed, was introduced to Britain during the 1880s from Asia. Although not the greatest of egg-layers (only around a hundred light-brown eggs a year can be expected from a happy hen because breeding for 'feather and fluff' has an impact on egg productiv-ity), the hens are excellent, broody birds, and also make good surrogate mothers, being quite pre-pared to hatch and raise other hens' chicks.

Large, deep- and short-bodied, Cochins look quite square in shape because their tail is small and is hardly visible. The plain-coloured varieties – black, white and buff – have beaks that are respec-tively rich yellow, yellow-horn-black and bright yellow in colour. The partridge variety has very pretty lacing on the back, wing and neck feathers, while the cuckoo variety has gorgeous, blue-grey bands across a lighter-blue-grey background. Not only is it good-looking, but the Cochin also has a terrific personality, being friendly, easy to handle and happy in most conditions. That said, Cochins are not good foragers, preferring instead to be kept

BLUE COCHIN HEN

BEAUTIFUL GOLDEN COCHIN

in nice, dry runs, although these large birds do need plenty of space.

The Cochin is such a handsome breed that these birds are hard to resist, being great big, cuddly giants that really do seem to like human company, enjoy being handled and are generally peaceful and docile. In addition, they don't mind being confined or roaming free, although note that their handsome, feathered feet and legs require special attention, and that Cochins should therefore also only be kept on clean, dry flooring. Despite this, Cochins are an excellent choice for the novice chicken-keeper, or for anyone who wants a bird that is reliably broody.

Croad Langshan

Originally from China, the Croad Langshan was brought to the UK from Langsham (in China) by a Major Croad during the 1870s. In Germany, breeders later crossed Major Croad's birds with Minorcas and Plymouth Rocks to increase egg capacity, and in so doing produced a separate breed: the Langsham.

Although it is not as popular as other Asiatic birds, the Croad Langshan is nonetheless an elegant breed that is available in just two colours: black and white. Because it has not been overbred for 'feather and fluff', the Croad Langshan retains much of its utility value, and the hens produce a reasonable number of medium-sized, dark-brown-coloured eggs that often have a pretty, plum-coloured bloom on their shells; the hens also make good brooders. On a practical level, these birds are quite easy to keep, being generally calm, and they would be a good choice for a family environment. They tolerate confinement well (note that the floor of their hencoop or run should be dry on account of their leg feathers), but they can be flighty, so must be enclosed by secure boundaries in order to keep them from fluttering off into a neighbour's garden. Both male and female Croad Langshans have five-pointed, single combs, but the males appear to have short backs because they carry their tails upright, forming a distinctive 'U' shape.

Dorking

Having been around at the time of the Roman invasion of Britain in AD 43, the Dorking is probably the oldest English breed of chicken. During the ninth century, the Dorking was crossed with many other breeds, including the French Crevecoeur, to improve its suitability as a table bird. Indeed, it now makes an excellent table bird: a large male can weigh up to 6.35 kg (14 lb), with large hens being a little smaller at 4.5 kg (10 lb).

The great peculiarities of this breed are, firstly, the five toes on each foot that bear a great, boat-shaped body, and, secondly, the colour variations that dictate the shape or type of comb: silver-grey, dark and red Dorkings have a single comb, while white and cuckoo varieties have a rose-type comb. Dorking hens lay around a hundred cream-coloured eggs a year (unless they are silver-grey or dark varieties, which lay white eggs, tinted eggs being the result of the breed having been crossed with the Sussex), but do so only during the spring and summer, not all year round. Docile in nature, Dorkings nevertheless need plenty of space, and prefer foraging on a free-ranging basis to being confined. The hens make good brooders, but Dorking chicks can be delicate and slow to develop; they are best hatched in spring so that the warm summer can help to build up their strength for the winter.

Faverolles

The Faverolles breed takes its name from the village in France where it was developed. It is thought to be the result of crossings between Cochins, Houdans and Dorkings, made in an attempt to produce a heavy table bird with a good egg-laying capacity, especially during the winter. This sturdy, dual-purpose bird arrived in England in 1886, where it was both appreciated in its own right and crossed with other breeds, such as the Sussex and Orpington.

Large, active and attractive birds – and good layers – Faverolles are easy birds to live with, but their docile nature has a downside in that they can be prone to bullying by other, more aggressive or assertive, breeds. The hens lay around a hundred smallish, light-brown eggs a year, and can make good broodies. Faverolles, which have a beard and whiskers, are available in a variety of colours: black, buff, white, salmon, cuckoo, ermine and laced blue. Like the Dorking, Faverolles have five toes on each foot. They stand on quite short, feathered legs, which means that their accommodation needs to be kept clean and dry.

White Dorking Rooster

Marans

The Marans (it always has an 's' at the end, even if you're referring to only a single bird) comes from the town of Marans, near La Rochelle in western France, and this is a fine, dual-purpose breed that is good for producing both eggs and meat. The Marans was developed during the 1920s, and its original make-up is thought to have included Croad Langshans, Malines, Faverolles and Barred Rocks, among other breeds.

Available in black (although this colour is quite rare) and dark, golden and silver cuckoo, it was the cuckoo forms that first came to Britain, probably because it is easy to tell the sex of birds of these colours at an early age. The cuckoo pattern is very pretty, the dark-cuckoo variety having blue-black banding across all of its parts; the golden cuckoo displaying black and gold on blue-grey; and the silver cuckoo having white feathering on the necks and generally appearing to be a lighter version of the dark cuckoo. All Marans have big, red-orange-coloured eyes, with large pupils, as well as a single comb with up to seven serrations. The Marans' most outstanding feature has to be the numerous rich, dark-chocolate-coloured eggs laid by the hens.

Marans prefer not to be handled, so may not suit a family with young children. They are also busy birds that prefer to roam free and to be allowed to peck away at garden pests rather than being confined to a run.

Orpington

The ideal beginner's bird, the Orpington is a big, cuddly breed that's friendly and docile: it will happily allow itself to be picked up and carried by children, but it can also be bullied by other breeds, so a close eye needs to be kept on these birds if they are maintained in mixed flocks. This gentle giant will reward its keeper with around 150 good-sized brown eggs in season (that is, during the spring and summer).

Originally bred during the 1880s by William Cook, and named after his hometown in Kent, it was the black variety of Orpington that emerged first, the result of a cross between Langshan, Mi-

PLYMOUTH ROCK, BARRED

norca and Plymouth Rock birds. Just eight years later came the white and buff forms, with the blue arriving during the 1920s. For show purposes, later breeders crossed the birds with Cochins to increase the 'feather and fluff' (the short legs are all but hidden by a mass of feathers), at the expense of the breed's laying capacity. Yet the Orpington remains a good dual-purpose bird, being a reasonable layer in season and making a good-sized table bird, with males' weight averaging at around 3.6 kg (8 lb).

Orpingtons like to forage around when given the chance, but will adapt to confinement quite well. It's a very hardy breed, and the hens make good mothers; and don't overlook the bantam versions if you have only a small space in which to keep chickens. In summary, whether a large fowl or a bantam version, the Orpington is a good choice for the novice poultry-keeper.

Plymouth Rock

A popular dual-purpose breed, the Plymouth Rock is an American breed that was first developed in Massachusetts during the 1820s. Its exact ancestral mix is still a bit of a mystery, however: Dominique males crossed with either Black Cochins or Java hens perhaps? The barred version appeared in 1874, with white and black variants following soon afterwards (as 'sport' fowl), after which came the buff (which was actually created in Rhode Island) and then other colours, including the Columbian. With their deep body, straight back, medium-sized tail, short, yellow beak and large eyes, they are very impressive looking birds, too, whatever their colour variation.

Plymouth Rock hens are good layers, producing 160 cream-coloured (described as 'yellowish' in the USA) eggs in season. They mature early, and can be quite greedy eaters, so take care not to overfeed them if they are kept within runs. They don't mind being confined, but enjoy a good forage when allowed to roam free. If there were a prize for personality, then Plymouth Rocks would probably win by a mile: these must be the friend-

which breeds? **163**

liest of all fowl, being really happy to be handled, placid and easily tamed, making them ideal pets.

Rhode Island Red

Known simply as the 'Rhode Island' in the USA, the suffix 'Red' is applied in Britain and other countries where a white variety is also to be found. The Rhode Island is an American composite breed that is valued for its egg production and meat-yielding qualities. The breed is the result of crossing native American breeds with imported breeds like Shanghais, Malays, Javas and Leghorns, a programme that began during the mid-nineteenth century. The first birds with rose combs were shown to the public in 1880 in Massachusetts, and the breed had been standardised in the USA by 1906. In 1909, the Rhode Island Red Club was established in Britain – and exists to this day (and if you are thinking of keeping this breed, then joining the club is a must!)

The Rhode Island Red is best described as oblong in shape, with a long, flat back and a slightly raised tail and vertical breast. Despite their name, these birds are not red, but a beautiful reddish-brown and black colour, with either a rose or a single, five-pointed comb and bright-yellow legs. Docile and calm, the Rhode Island Red is an ideal backyard chicken – although note that the males can get a bit aggressive with each other – as it will either adapt to confinement within runs as long as there's plenty of space (which is true for all breeds) or will happily roam free. It's the Rhode Island Red's egg production that really sets it apart from other breeds: expect around two hundred large, brown eggs in season. Apart from the fact that the hens don't generally become broody (which makes raising chicks a bit difficult as this consequently needs to be done in incubators), the Rhode Island Red scores top marks as both a beginner's bird and an egg-layer.

Sussex

When the Romans arrived in Britain in AD 43, the Sussex was prized for its meat. The ever-popular Sussex is now a dual-purpose bird: by the nineteenth century, the original, white-fleshed table

LIGHT SUSSEX   SILVER-LACED WYANDOTTE ROOSTER

fowl had been crossed with newly imported Asiatic breeds like the Brahma, and it was shown in its present form at Britain's first poultry show in 1845. A Sussex hen will lay around 180 good-sized eggs in season, while a large male can reach about 4.1 kg (9 lb) in weight.

The Sussex can be described as a classic-looking breed, being neat and well proportioned, with a tail held at an angle of 45 degrees and a single, vertical comb that's evenly serrated. These birds are available in a variety of colours, including brown, red, white, light (which has pretty, black-striped hackle feathers, a white body and a black tail), buff (which is similar to the light but with a rich, golden-buff hue), silver and speckled (essentially a rich mahogany colour, with each feather being striped with black and tipped with white). Docile, gentle, and easy to handle, as well as an active and curious bird, the Sussex is difficult to fault, both as a large fowl and in bantam form: it's a wonderful breed, suited to novices and seasoned poultry-keepers alike.

Wyandotte

If you want a very attractive bird that's hardy, has a terrific temperament and is one of the best layers around – expect around 200 eggs in a hen's first year, dropping to only 175 in her second – then the Wyandotte is the breed for you. These chickens are easy to keep on a day-to-day basis (but note that they can gain weight if they are overfed), and will happily forage or live in confinement.

The Wyandotte is a comparatively young, dual-purpose breed that was developed in the USA. The silver-laced version (the best layer of all) was produced in New York State by crossing a Sebright cock with the offspring of a silver-spangled Hamburgh male and Cochin hen. After further breeding, the breed was put before the American Standards Committee in 1876 as an 'American Sebright', but was rejected because the head and comb shapes were considered to be wrong. More crossbreeding followed, with Brahmas and silver-laced Polands, until, in 1883, the breed was standardised as the Wyandotte (the name of a tribe of First Nation people). Today, 14 colour variations are recognised in the UK, with some 22 in total being recognised around the world – including barred, black, blue, blue-laced, buff, buff-laced, Columbian, gold-laced, red, partridge, silver-laced, silver-pencilled and white – all with a lovely, curvy body and a deep breast. It's not just their variety that makes them popular birds, but also their ease of keeping and their fantastic egg production. Bantam versions are also available.

RARE BREEDS

The following breeds fall into the rare-breed category.

Campine

Originating in the Campine region of Belgium (to the east of Antwerp), but also from the Dutch province of North Brabant, the Campine is a compact bird; large males weigh on average 2.7 kg (6 lb), and large hens, about 2.25 kg/5 lb, with bantams being a quarter of the size. It is an interesting breed because the colour markings of both male and female birds are virtually identical – the males being 'hen-feathered', that is, they lack the usual,

more pronounced hackle, sickle and saddle feathers – but the two are distinguished by their combs: the female's single comb falls to one side, while the male's remains erect. They also both have quite long, lovely, blue-coloured legs. The neck feathers are pure white in the silver version, making a gorgeous-looking 'cape', while the white cape is golden-coloured in the gold version. The rest of the body is white, with beetle-green barring on all feathers.

Despite being alert and lively birds, Campines are not particularly friendly in nature, but do vary in temperament: some individuals are aloof, others, quite approachable. Campines are good layers of white, medium-sized eggs, as well as being fine foragers, early-feathering and fast-maturing birds. Like all of the light European breeds, they are very active, and therefore need plenty of space, although they will tolerate confinement if necessary.

Houdan

Introduced into the UK from France during the mid-nineteenth century, the Houdan hails from the region just to the east of Paris. Its striking and unusual appearance – five toes on each foot, and an impressive head crest – betrays its originator breeds: the Poland and the Dorking. Available in

the chicken keeper's handbook

both large-fowl and bantam sizes, this rare breed needs a lot of attention: the head-crest feathers suffer in wet or freezing conditions, and the hens are neither good 'broodies' nor great layers (130 to 140 quite small, white eggs in season). Nevertheless, these active birds – who enjoy foraging, but adapt well to confinement – are very docile and friendly, making them easy to handle. In addition, its rich, black feathering, which is mottled with white over most of its body, coupled with a beard and whiskers (not to mention the pompom-like crest), make this a most attractive bird.

Jersey Giant

A giant among chickens – large males can reach a massive 5.9 kg (13 lb) in weight, and even the hens can weigh as much as 4.55 kg (10 lb) – like other large breeds, Jersey Giants are very gentle and docile birds that are easily handled and are therefore well suited to the domestic environment. Their sheer size means that you need to think about and plan their housing well in advance of their arrival, though. These birds need space, but, surprisingly, are not good foragers, instead preferring confinement and feeding (and this should be measured so that they don't become overweight). The hens are good layers, producing around 180 brown-shelled, medium-sized eggs a year, and they also make good mothers, although their size can cause them unwittingly to break their eggs as they sit on them. Note that Jersey Giants are slow to mature: birds reared for the table will need about six months in which to reach their full size.

Available in black, blue and white (and in bantam-sized versions of all of these colours), the breed was developed not in the Channel Islands, but in the USA – in New Jersey – during the late nineteenth century as a dual-purpose bird created by breeding Dark Brahmas, Black Javas, Black Langshans and Cornish game (Indian game) birds. Because Jersey Giants are slow developers, commercial breeders weren't interested in birds that didn't fatten up quickly, and so the breed languished. It was also thought that American backyard poultry-keepers didn't much care for black chickens with dark legs (curiously, the bottoms of their feet are yellow), which is a shame, because the Black Jersey Giant has gorgeous black plumage shot with a green sheen, while the blue version has a laced pattern to its feathers. This is a breed that has plenty to offer, and that deserves much more attention than it receives at the moment.

Marsh Daisy

In 1880, John Wright, of Marshside, in Lancashire, began chicken-breed-ing experiments, crossing White Leghorns, Malays, Black Hamburghs and Old English game birds to produce a fowl that was suited to his needs. Once established, the breed was kept isolated from further crossbreeding for thirty years, until it became standardised. In 1913, Charles Moore, from Doncaster, Yorkshire, bought two of the last hens from Wright, mated them with a pit-game (fighting) cock and later introduced a Sicilian But-tercup to the genetic mix. And in 1922, the breed was admitted to the poultry standards under the delightful name of Marsh Daisy. Having been popular for a number of years, the breed then faded into obscurity, and was thought to have died out, until, in 1971, a flock was discovered in Somerset. The breed was subsequently revived, and since then the Marsh Daisy has been slowly growing in popularity, especially among small-holders.

The Marsh Daisy is easy to keep, has a nice, calm temperament, and the hens lay a good number of smallish, white-shelled eggs. Although the breed can be kept in confinement, it really prefers to range around freely (but note that it may fly if disturbed by predators). When it comes to looks, the Marsh Daisy has all of the key points that make for an attractive, tra-ditional-looking bird. Black, white, brown, buff, wheaten and white ver-sions are available, and the birds grow to a good size, with a lovely, plump breast. The earlobes are often a combination of red and white – but are always more red than white – and the eyes are red, too. The head is topped by an impressive rose comb that is evenly spiked, and that has a single leader that sticks out towards the back. The longish neck is covered in lovely hackle

feathers, which fall downwards to form a 'cape' around the shoulders (and the brown and wheaten versions display perhaps the most attractive colour combinations of rich gold, black and brown). This rare breed (there is no bantam-sized version) is well worth seeking out for its utility and good looks, so scour the poultry press for reputable, established breeders, and when you are lucky enough to find some, be prepared to wait because these birds are slow to mature.

New Hampshire Red

Developed as a dual-purpose breed directly from the Rhode Island Red by farmers in the American state of New Hampshire, who spent thirty years or so refining the original breed rather than embarking on complex crossbreeding programmes, the New Hampshire Red was finally 'perfected' in 1935. In spite of being a formidable layer – one trial bird was recorded as producing 332 eggs in a 52-week period! – the New Hampshire Red lan-

guished in the shadow of its 'parent' breed until the 1980s, when a bantam version was introduced and interest in the breed overall began to grow.

To the original breeders, its eggs were more important than its looks, but the New Hampshire Red wins many a heart with its red-brown-coloured homeliness. Its well-rounded, deep body makes it look just as a chicken should, and the addition of a five-pointed comb, oval-shaped red earlobes and rich-yellow legs makes for picture-book poultry. The male birds have lovely, black tail feathers and some black edging on the wing feathers, while the hens have black tips to the feathers on the lower neck and dark edges on the wing and tail feathers. Although egg production isn't as great as it once was, a happy hen will still produce around 140 eggs in a season. In terms of personality, New Hampshire Reds are friendly, docile and ideally suited to life in a back yard, where they will adapt to being confined, but will forage happily if allowed to do so. As a large, heavy breed – and not a very active one at that –

note that New Hampshires can gain weight if fed too much.

Norfolk Grey

Friendliness, docility, great maternal instincts and striking good looks are all combined in the Norfolk Grey, a rare breed that deserves much greater attention than it currently receives. Developed in Norfolk, England, during the early twentieth century by Fred Myhill, of Norwich, as a utility bird, it never caught on, and during the 1970s there were just four birds left. Thankfully, the breed was saved, and today its future is assured – and rightly so, for this is a magnificent breed in terms of both looks and temperament.

The Norfolk Grey has a long body and wide shoulders, a great, full breast and a well-feathered tail. The males have the most wonderful silver-white feathering, with black striping on their necks, while the rest of the bird is black. The hens are similar, but with some silver lacing on the breast; they are reasonable layers of medium-sized brown eggs, can go broody and make excellent mothers. Norfolk Greys are a hardy breed, ideally suited to foraging, but also adapt to confinement.

North Holland Blue

The North Holland Blue is a very good rare breed to search out if you are looking for attractive birds that have tasty meat and that are great layers, too: a young, healthy hen will easily lay 180 eggs each season, and some will lay even more (up to 220 eggs). Bantam versions are also available. Quiet, friendly and docile birds, they make great additions to the family.

This Dutch breed is the result of crosses between Belgian Malines, Plymouth Rocks, the Sussex, Orpingtons and Rhode Island Reds during the late nineteenth and early twentieth centuries, and the result is a very attractive bird, with an all-over blue-grey cuckoo plumage pattern carried on a compact, upright body, and widely spaced, lightly feathered legs. North Holland Blues have short beaks and very bold, red-orange eyes that make them look interested in things around them. These birds love to forage, but if you are keeping them in confinement, be careful not to overfeed them as they can easily put on weight. The North Holland Blue is a breed that you'll need to seek out, but it's well worth looking for.

Vorwerk

At the beginning of the twentieth century, German poultry-breeder Oskar Vorwerk set out to breed a rich-buff-coloured bird that also had the solid black neck hackle found in the Lakenvelder breed. Using Buff Orpingtons to obtain the colour that he wanted, as well as Lakenvelders, Andalusians and Buff Ramelslohers, Vorwerk was aiming for a good-quality utility breed that matured early and that was a bit fleshier than other farmyard breeds found in Germany at the time. The results came in 1912, in the form of the breed bearing his name: the Vorwerk. After all of that hard work, the breed nearly died out after World War II, but was revived from just a handful of the remaining birds. It was introduced to Britain in 1970, the bantam form following in 1997 (since then, a blue version of the bantam has been developed). Although kept by only a handful of enthusiastic poultry-keepers, the breed's future seems secure. It is looked after in Britain by the Rare Poultry Society, the first point of call for anyone interested in raising the Vorwerk (or, indeed, any other rare poultry breed), who is in need of information and advice.

The breed is just what Vorwerk wanted: a chicken that is practical to keep – ideal for the novice poultry-keeper – as well as being a good layer and fast to mature. Male birds that are raised together will get along in adulthood, but note that bantam males can be aggressive and are not suited to homes where there are children (large-fowl males are generally good-tempered, though).

CHAPTER EIGHT
Hatching and despatching

Once you have kept chickens for a while and have enjoyed their eggs, your thoughts may turn to increasing the number of birds that you own. You could, of course, buy some additional point of lay (POL) hens, or you may want to increase your flock naturally, by hatching and rearing fertilised eggs. On the other hand, you may also be faced with what to do with ageing birds that have come to the end of their productive laying life or that are males who are surplus to your requirements or else have been specifically reared for eating. Both the start and the end of a chicken's life are important considerations for the poultry enthusiast.

Hatching options

There are four basic ways by which a flock can be increased. Firstly, the flock can be increased in size by the purchase and introduction of new birds; these could be day-old chicks or point of lay hens, depending on what you need. Secondly, you could allow nature to do the work and could introduce a cockerel to the flock; he could be borrowed or, indeed, rented for the sole purpose of mating with the hens, after which you could let

your 'girls' sit on their eggs, hatch them and rear them. An alternative to getting in a cockerel is to buy ready fertilised eggs that broody hens can sit on and hatch, thereby acting as surrogate mothers to a clutch. Finally, you could go down the technological route and could buy ready fertilised eggs for you to hatch and rear using an incubator, heat lamps and other equipment with which to bring on the chicks.

In the 'wild'

A hen herself hatches as a chick with a finite number of eggs cells already within her ovaries, and they govern the number of eggs that she produces over the course of her laying life. A hen's first-year laying season will be her most productive, and while she will lay bigger eggs in her second year, there will be fewer of them. During her third and fourth years, a hen's laying productivity falls even further (commercial hens aren't kept for longer than two years, and often for only one year until

their first moult, when they stop laying altogether). As a hen ages, the number of eggs that she produces diminishes further; a healthy, happy hen can live to be nine or ten years old, but she may well not be producing any eggs at all by this time.

In their prime, hens will lay an egg a day until they have produced a good-sized clutch – anything between six and fifteen eggs – and will then stop laying and become broody. A broody hen will sit on these eggs, providing them with the heat needed to incubate the embryos inside. For large breeds of chickens, this sitting process takes around 21 days, and for bantams, two or three days less. During this time, the broody hen will not leave her nesting box, but will turn the eggs regularly and will reposition them beneath her so that all are kept snug and warm.

In the domestic situation, it's this desire to produce a clutch that keeps the hen laying on a daily basis: as long as the eggs are removed, the hen will continue to lay, and may not become broody at all. Furthermore, the hen doesn't need a male bird in order to lay eggs for consumption, and can manage quite well on her own. If you want to raise chicks, though, you will need a male bird to fertilise the eggs.

BROODY BIRDS

Some breeds of chickens are more prone to going broody than others: Silkies, for example (whose sole purpose in life seems to be to raise a clutch), go broody quite often. Other breeds, by contrast, don't get the urge quite so strongly, and, indeed, some make rather negligent mothers. Hybrid birds aren't very good sitters, and some of the light breeds, like the Leghorn, are also not good at this. The best breeds for broodiness are to be found among the heavy, docile birds, such as the Sussex, Orpington, Brahma, Rhode Island Red and Plymouth Rock. Even so, trying to predict when a hen will go broody is a bit hit and miss, but you can just about guarantee that she will at some stage.

A BIT OF ENCOURAGEMENT

If you want a hen to lay a clutch, you may need to give her a bit of help to encourage her to get in the mood to go broody, in which case put half-a-dozen ceramic or rubber eggs in the sitting box – even nice, smooth stones may work – but don't use real eggs as they could get broken, may start the hen egg-eating or may just go stale. Then position both the hen and the box away from the other hens to give her privacy; you could also add a little maize to her feed ration.

The whole process of getting a hen broody may take two or three weeks, so you'll need to be patient, and chances are that while you're waiting for one hen, a different hen will take it into her head to go broody! Note that getting a hen to become broody using fake eggs means that you could later substitute real, ready fertilised eggs for the fakes, which the foster hen could then hatch and raise.

LOOK FOR THE SIGNS

The next step is to keep an eye open for the telltale signs of broodiness. A broody hen will start to spend a lot more time in her nesting box, for example, and if she sits in it at night, then that's a sure sign that she's broody. She may also start to raise her feathers when you get close to her. If you lift her out of her nest, she will make a characteristic 'clock-clock-clock' sound, and you should also see that she has lost some of the feathers around her breast. And if you then place her on the ground, she will probably spread out her wings and get a bit angry with you, which is not really surprising as she wants to get back to her eggs.

EXERCISE IS IMPORTANT, BUT SO IS COMFORT

Despite the broody hen's desire to sit on her eggs forever, she does need to be lifted out of her box for twenty to thirty minutes each day in order to feed, exercise and defecate. This can be done in the morning or evening, but a routine must be established about one week before she starts sitting on a clutch, especially if you decide to place ready fertilised eggs underneath her. (In this case, the eggs need to be cleaned first with a special disinfectant.)

A comfortable hen is more likely to have success in raising a clutch. She therefore needs to be flea- and mite-free, so a good dusting of an appropriate preventative powder is advised. In addition, she should be settled in a place that is secure and peaceful, so that she feels relaxed.

Many purpose-built nesting boxes are floorless, the idea being that the moisture from the earth helps to keep the eggs surrounded by a humid atmosphere under the hen's body. Humidity levels inside the nesting box (and also in an incubator, see below, pages 183 to 189) control the amount of fluid that evaporates from inside the egg, and remember that the presence of fluid is vital to the developing chick. As for feeding, wheat and fresh water should always be available to a sitting hen, along with grit.

If the nesting box is not floorless, however, then you'll need to raise the humidity level by sprinkling each egg with just 2 or 3 – no more – drops of clean water heated to blood temperature towards the end of the hatching period (on days 18, 19 and 20 for large breeds of fowl, and days 16, 17 and 18 for bantams). Always sprinkle the water on the eggs just before the hen returns to the nest after her break, to avoid chilling them.

It's vital that the hen defecates during her exercise period because soiling the nest contaminates the eggs. If she does this, you'll need to remove the dirty nesting material and provide a clean and fresh replacement. Finally, remember that she'll really appreciate a dust-bath during her exercise break.

The happy hatch

The mother hen needs to be left in peace on the day that her eggs hatch, with any disturbances being kept to a minimum. So if you lift her to check on progress, make sure that you do this very gently, and that you check carefully to ensure that no newborn chicks are tucked under her wings (where it's nice and warm). But even after hatching has started, the hen still needs her daily break, so while she's away from the nest, lay a towelling face flannel over the top of it to keep the chicks warm and lessen the sound of their cheeping. Their calls will draw the hen back to the nest, which is why muffling them a bit will allow her to take her break without being too concerned about their well-being. As the chicks hatch, remove the discarded shells so that they don't get stuck over the ends of eggs that have yet to hatch, thus creating a double wall of shell that a chick has to break through. Any eggs that don't hatch should similarly be removed and discarded.

INTO THE BROODY COOP

Once the newly hatched chicks have dried out and fluffed up, they and their mother should be transferred to a broody coop containing litter consisting of wood-shavings (straw becomes tangled around little chicks' legs). Place a very shallow dish of proprietary chick crumb in the coop, and the hen should then teach the chicks to feed (don't be alarmed if she also scratches litter into the food – this is normal). The chicks need water, too, and when providing it, make sure that you use a proper chick font so that there is no danger of the little birds drowning.

The hen and her chicks should remain confined within the broody coop for about a week, but if the weather is good, you could let the chicks into a small run next to the coop. Keep the hen out for the first week, however. After three weeks, the hen and her chicks will need a larger run, but note that this should not be too big because the chicks may tire easily, and may then lose their body heat and become chilled. Also remember that the chicken family must be shut in securely at night.

The hen will stay with the chicks for six to eight weeks, after which time she can be returned to her normal pen with the other adult birds. She may start to moult at this point – this may come as a bit of a shock to the first-time poultry-keeper, but it is quite normal.

Using an incubator

Hatching eggs artificially, using an incubator, is a viable alternative for many poultry-keepers who do not have the space or facilities to assist the natural process. Incubators may come in all shapes and sizes (and with greatly differing prices, too), but all replicate the natural environment created by a sitting hen. At the bottom end of the market – in terms of price and gizmos – are 'still-air' incubators. These consist largely of an electric light bulb that provides the heat for incubation. (Note that the new, low-energy light bulbs are not suitable for this purpose as they do not produce heat in the same way as old-fashioned, incandescent light bulbs.) More expensive incubators come with a range of fans and heating elements, and are generally called 'forced-air' incubators.

An incubator's vital component is heat, but the poultry-keeper still has a hands-on role, even when using the fanciest of machines, because the eggs have to be turned regularly during the incubation period. Each egg, lying on its long side, has to be rotated through 180 degrees at least three times (and preferably five times) every day. Always pick an odd number of rotations so that the eggs don't end up in the same position at night. The eggs in the incubator have to be turned for the first 18 days of incubation; forgetting to do this can be a disaster, and is probably the biggest cause of egg death. The simplest way to ensure that you turn all of the eggs is to mark each shell with a cross on one side, thereby creating a visible reminder to help you ascertain that you have turned over the egg. Alternatively, you could invest in a sophisticated incubator with a built-in egg-rotator, which may be either semi-automatic or fully automatic.

TEMPERATURE CONTROL

Just as, in nature, eggs lie under a warm, feathery hen (a bit like lying under a living duvet), so eggs in an incubator need to be kept warm. Still-air incubators should run at 39.4°C (103°F), and forced-air incubators at a very slightly cooler 37.7°C (100°F). A good thermometer is therefore vital. Readings should be taken at the top of the eggs, as they lie in the tray.

It's also important that you take care where you site the incubator. Don't put it in a hot, heated room or in a cold shed or garage: instead, the best location in which to keep temperature levels throughout the hatching period constant is a spare room, with any radiators switched off. Even a slight variation in temperature – say, of 1°C – can have an impact on the number of eggs that are successfully hatched. Run the incubator for 24 hours before you place any eggs in it in order to give it a test-run and to make sure that the unit is clean (clean it inside and out with a proprietary incubator disinfectant). Be prepared for some disappointment, though: successful hatching – be it when a live hen is sitting on her clutch, or in a top-of-the-range incubator – cannot be guaranteed.

SELECTING EGGS

Remember that eggs will only hatch in an incubator – or under a foster hen – if they are fertilised, and that you can buy fertilised eggs by mail order or over the internet (postal delivery may, however, cause some breakages, so it's often best to pick them up from a local breeder yourself).

Fertilised eggs, be they laid by your own hens or purchased from a poultry-breeder, should be as fresh as possible (and never more than a week old) when put into an incubator. The eggs must also be clean (the warmth of the incubator provides a perfect breeding ground for any bacteria and viruses that may otherwise be present), so use a proprietary egg-wash to prepare the eggs. Avoid any defective eggs – those with cracked or misshapen shells (either elongated, like a sausage, or too round, like a golf ball) – and reject any that are too large or too small, too. Instead, stick to oval-

FERTILISED EGGS SHOULD BE AS FRESH AS POSSIBLE.

shaped eggs with a pointed and a blunt end, weighing around 55 g (2 oz).

FERTILE OR NOT?

You can only tell if an egg is fertile after it has been in the incubator for ten days. The technique used for seeing if it is fertile is called candling, and it's quite easy to carry out. Just shine a bright light – a torch, perhaps – at the egg, and you should then be able to see what's going on inside. If the egg is fertile and developing normally, you will see a spidery pattern of blood vessels emerging from the dark, central spot of the embryo. If the egg is infertile, or the embryo has died, the egg will appear to be completely clear. Infertile eggs should be removed from the incubator (they are no different to the eggs laid by a hen on a daily basis, so you could eat them).

HUMIDITY

A further influencing factor regarding whether an egg develops and hatches successfully is humidity. All incubators have a water tray, but how and when it should be filled varies from model to model, so read the instructions for your machine carefully.

Monitoring the amount and speed of fluid evaporation from the egg within the incubator can be done by candling: shine the torch or a light at the egg and look at the air sac at the blunt end of the egg. In a fresh egg, the air sac will take up a slice across the top of the blunt end, and this should grow bigger as the embryo develops and the fluid inside the egg evaporates through the shell. Seven days later, the air sac should have grown to take up about one-sixth of the blunt end; fourteen days later, it should be about a quarter of the size of the egg, or about 2.5 cm (1 in) deep. Just before hatching, the air sac should equate to a good one-third of the egg in size. Don't be alarmed if the air sac's level is slightly off, that is, if it does not pass straight across the blunt end, but dips to one side a little – this is normal.

If you think that the air sac is looking a little too small during the incubation process, this means that the humidity level within the incubator is a bit too high, and that the water needs to be removed for a day or so. If, on the other hand, you think that the air space is becoming too big, you'll need to add some more water to raise the humidity level.

THE BIG BREAK-OUT

Hatching should occur on day 21. (Note that it's important that you don't turn the eggs during their last three days in the incubator because the chicks inside are fully developed, so that turning them around would be like subjecting them to a ride on a rollercoaster!) Before this happens, make sure that the humidity level within the incubator is kept up to prevent the shells' membranes from drying out and becoming too hard, trapping the chicks inside the shells as a result. The chicks will then chip their way out of the shells (a process known as 'pipping'). Any eggs that haven't hatched can be left for 24 hours (but no longer), and those that fail to hatch after this time must be discarded and disposed of.

The newly emerged chicks will have eaten the remains of the yolk in the egg, which will sustain them for the first two days of their lives. Now leave the newly hatched chicks in the incubator for 24 hours to dry out and fluff up. After that time, they should feel soft, but firm. Note that if chicks feel dry, it means that the humidity level was either a bit too low, or the temperature a little too high, during incubation. Conversely, chicks that feel 'sticky' (known as 'drowned') point to too high a humidity level or too low a temperature. If you notice any of these, make a mental note that you should make some tiny, yet important, adjustments next time around.

Once hatched and dried, the chicks must be moved out of the incubator and into their new home. This stage is critical because they must learn to drink and eat as soon as possible. And with no mother hen to teach them how, that duty falls to their keeper.

THE BROODY ENCLOSURE

Just as a hen is moved with her chicks into a broody coop, so chicks that have just hatched in an incubator also go through a brooding stage, this being the first month of their lives, after which they pass on to their growing, or rearing, stage. This lasts until the birds are 18 weeks old, at which point hens reach their point of lay (POL) stage and start laying eggs of their own. The young chicks are very vulnerable during the brooding period: disease and chills are the main threats to their lives, and transferring them to a broody enclosure will help to ensure that they are raised in isolation, as well as in a temperature-controlled environment.

You can keep the chicks confined within a shed or a section of a coop by using a 'corral' made of cardboard. When they grow a little older and need more space, you can simply move the walls of the corral outwards a bit. The chicks also need litter in their enclosure: use clean, white wood-shavings (not hay or straw) spread to a depth of about 5–8 cm (2–3 in). Then lay an old towel or sheet of cardboard (corrugated would be the best) on top so that the chicks can learn to find their feet: the firmer surface will help them to stand up and move around, and it can be removed when they become sturdier and confident about walking.

The broody enclosure will need a heat source to keep the chicks warm, too. If there are just a few chicks, then a 60-watt light bulb suspended above a large cardboard box, or else fixed within an upside-down terracotta plant pot situated in the centre of the corral, should do the job. If you have more chicks, you will need a more efficient heat source than this light-bulb lamp, such as a gas-powered heater (or an electric one if you have a power source nearby) or an infrared lamp. The temperature around the floor area where the chicks are being kept needs to be about 32°C (90°F), so it's important

to keep an eye on the thermometer, especially at around midday, when the ambient temperature in the shed or sectioned-off area of the coop may be higher. If the chicks cluster together under the lamp, then they are still feeling a bit cold, so drop the height of the light bulb a little to radiate more heat. If the chicks have arranged themselves around the edges of the box, however, then they are too warm, so raise the height of the bulb a little. You should progressively raise the height of the lamp each week until, by the end of the third week, the temperature at floor level is around 21°C (70°F).

When the chicks are three weeks old, weather permitting, you can switch off the heat lamp during the day. You could also take the chicks outside and put them in a small wire pen on the grass to let them take the air for the first time. Make sure that this pen is completely cat-proof: the 'holes' in the chicken-wire sides must be quite small lest a paw be squeezed through and a chick grabbed. Also note that you should place the pen in the shade so that the chicks don't become over-heated, and that you must take them inside straightaway should it start to rain.

Keep the brooding pen well lit during the day to replicate daylight, and encourage the chicks to feed and drink. But remember that too much light will overstimulate them, while too dim a light will make them lethargic and will affect their overall growth rate because they won't then eat so well.

TEACHING CHICKS TO FEED AND FEEDING CHICKS

The feeders and drinking vessels in artificial brooding enclosures need to be placed under, or close to, the heat source so that the chicks don't have far to go to find them. They probably won't eat anything during the first 24 hours of their lives, having come out of their eggs having just feasted on the remains of the yolk, but it's vital that they drink. To help them get used to eating, you may have to show them how to do it by jabbing your finger into the chick crumb: with luck, they'll think that you're a big mother hen pecking at the food, and will follow suit. For the only time in their lives, you could encourage the birds to eat by sprinkling a little very finely chopped hard-boiled egg over their feed: they'll be familiar with egg from their days in the shell, and it will give them a little extra protein over the first days of their lives. Don't mix up too much feed, though: just like wet mash for older birds, chick crumb will become stale, so remove any leftovers promptly.

Once the chicks are feeding, they should spend the next eight weeks eating chick crumb (which is sometimes also called 'chick starter ration'). This is chicken food in the form of crushed pellets, making it easier for little beaks to manage, and is usually medicated, too, to protect them from coccidiosis, at least until they have built up their own immunity levels. If the chicks are raised with a broody hen, don't be alarmed if she eats the chicks' food, too: this is natural, and if you try to give her adult-sized food, she will only pick it up and offer it to her chicks. At six weeks, note that the chicks will need flint grit; ordinary poultry grit is fine as the chicks will pick out the smaller bits, but you could also use grit specially milled for bantams, which is somewhat smaller.

Sexing chicks

In many breeds, it's impossible to tell whether a baby chick is male or female until it has grown significantly, although some pure breeds have

been specially developed to create what are called 'autosexing' breeds. In the case of these autosexed birds, their genes have been manipulated so that male and female birds are different colours when they hatch. This is useful because you will know from a very early stage how many females (who will become layers) you have, and how many males, which may be surplus to your requirements unless you want to rear them for breeding or for the table.

Some of the ways in which the sex of non-autosexed birds may be determined include:

•   examining combs and wattles because cockerels start to develop these before pullets;
•   examining their legs because pullets have less well-developed legs than cockerels;
•   examining the developing saddle feathers because in cockerels, the feathers near the tail and over the back are pointed in shape (a pullet's are rounded), and they also appear glossier;
•   looking at the feathers on the breast and back because males with partridge patterning often show a glimpse of their adult feather colouration in these areas at quite a young age;
•   listening to their voices because male birds often have a whining – some call it petulant – tone; and at 10 to 12 weeks of age (and sometimes even earlier), the giveaway sound is the crowing of a cockerel;
•   observing their behaviour because males often seem bolder, and may indulge in play-fighting (pullets may do the same, but less frequently).

Note that it is possible to end up with a batch of birds that are all the same sex. If you suspect that this has happened, then you will just have to wait until they are mature enough and developing their secondary characteristics before you can be sure.

the chicken keeper's handbook

Growers

Eight-week-old chicks are termed 'growers', and their food should now be changed from chick crumb to a lower-protein food called growers' rations (this should be introduced slowly to avoid upsetting a chick's digestive system). Once the birds have reached this stage, it's usually pretty clear what sex they are, and decisions will now have to be made as to their future.

When they are 12 weeks old, separate the cockerels and pullets so that the pullets can more easily be switched over to layers' rations when they are 16 to 18 weeks of age. The cockerels can either continue on growers' pellets or can be switched to finishing pellets in order to fatten them up, ready for the table. Separating the males from the females will also help you to ascertain whether you have made a mistake in sexing any of the birds.

Keeping chickens for meat

Keeping them for eggs is one of the main reasons for keeping chickens, and if you have hatched new birds to augment or replace older hens that have stopped laying, or have raised a surplus of cockerels, then you need to consider despatching some of them. Remember that some breeds have, indeed, been developed for their meat, and others, for their egg-laying capabilities, but that there are also several good dual-purpose breeds. That said, all healthy birds, regardless of their sex, can be eaten, although the older the birds, the tougher their meat is likely to be, so rather than an oven, a stew pot should be their final destination. Depending on the breed, most chickens will be 'oven-ready' at about five months of age.

DESPATCHING BIRDS

When the time comes to reduce the number of your birds, there are a few things that you need to do to prepare both the bird that you've decided to cull and yourself for the process. A number of courses are now offered by experienced poultry-keepers on culling and dressing birds. Attending one of these would be ideal because you will be shown the legal methods of culling, and, by watching an expert, you will become a lot more confident about doing it yourself. And being confident generally means that the process is much more speedy and efficient, so check your poultry magazine or club for details of courses near you. Alternatively, you could get an experienced chicken-keeper to cull your bird for you.

Having identified the bird that you want to cull, separate it from the rest of the flock, if possible the night beforehand, and house it in either a separate coop or a covered crate or box. This is partly so that the bird has time to calm down and partly to avoid disturbing the rest of the flock (and remember that the culling of a bird must take place well away from, and out of sight and out of sound of, the rest of the flock). To ensure that the bird's crop is empty (which makes dressing it a little easier), you should remove any food from the bird's pen, although drinking water should still be available to it. Then, the next morning, the bird should be despatched as quickly, painlessly and humanely as possible.

METHODS OF DESPATCH

A recognised and legal method of culling a chicken is neck-pulling, or neck dislocation (cervical dislocation), as it is often called. When this technique is carried out correctly, it instantaneously renders the bird unconscious, and the damage to the brainstem causes a very swift death. Neck-pulling by small-scale poultry-keepers is acceptable, but only when undertaken by someone with experience who is confident of performing the technique quickly and effectively because dislocating the neck can be hard to do, especially where some of the larger breeds of birds are concerned. An experienced slaughterer should be able to dislocate the neck and kill the bird without tearing the head from the neck.

Although it is rarely used, decapitation is another method of despatching a chicken. Indeed, the phrase 'running around like a headless chicken' does hold true: remove a chicken's head from its body, and it will continue to flap its wings, while blood from the wound will be sprayed over quite a distance. The severed head will furthermore often continue to open and close its beak and blink its eyes. All such body movements that occur shortly after death are, in fact, the result of nerve impulses.

When it comes to neck-crushing, note that although many poultry-suppliers sell specially designed pliers that are marketed as 'humane despatchers', these are actually not recognised as being humane by the Humane Slaughter Association (HSA).

The HSA does, however, recommend two methods of slaughter: the percussive method and electrical stunning. With the former method, a mechanical, cartridge-powered device produces a concussive blow, causing the death of the chicken. Used correctly, this method is one of the most reliable and humane methods, being more effective at disrupting brain function than either neck dislocation or crushing. Under current legislation, however, the percussive method must be followed by either neck-cutting or neck dislocation if the culling is for commercial purposes or a non-emergency culling (that is, when a bird is ill or injured and needs putting down). Hand-held electrical stunners are most commonly used by larger-scale, or commercial, poultry-producers. When carried out correctly, the stunning immediately renders the bird unconscious, and it is then killed by being bled before the bird recovers consciousness (so that loss of blood is the cause of death, not the initial stunning).

Although the two methods recommended by the HSA are the preferred humane methods of culling chickens, many small-scale poultry-keepers who need to cull their birds only infrequently may be put off by the cost of buying the necessary equipment. In this instance, it is far better either to arrange for birds to be culled by an experienced slaughterer or to pool resources with say, fellow members of a poultry club.

Whatever method of slaughter is used, and in all instances, remember that the cull should be carried out as quickly, effectively and humanely as possible.

PLUCKING BIRDS

With experience, it is possible to kill a bird by means of neck dislocation and not to rip the skin or head from the neck of the animal. When broken in this manner, the severed blood vessels will cause blood to pool within the bird's body. Hanging the dead bird by its feet will then cause the blood to pool in the head. Before doing this, however, you will need to remove the dead bird's feathers. Note that a newly killed bird's body will be warm and floppy for about forty-five minutes before rigor mortis sets in, and that you should therefore start plucking the bird as soon as possible after death.

Many people advise placing the dead bird in an old sack to collect the feathers while you are plucking them. Start by plucking the wing flight feathers and the tail feathers as these are harder

to remove when the bird is cold. Then pluck the legs and work your way forwards, plucking the feathers in the direction of growth rather than against it to avoid tearing the skin. When you get to the breast area, whose skin is quite delicate and tears easily, press the thumb of your free hand against the skin at the base of each feather as you pull it with the other hand. If the bird was killed at the start of its moult, underneath the plumage you will find hundreds of tiny pin feathers – new feathers that were waiting to grow to replace the old ones as they dropped – these can be fiddly to remove, but come away much more easily when the bird is cold. Any left on the skin can be singed off just before the bird is placed in the oven.

HANGING BIRDS

The next stage after plucking a chicken is hanging it. The bird's carcass should now be suspended by the legs somewhere cool (where it should also be protected from flies and other vermin). This allows the blood to drain fully into the broken neck cavity and makes the flesh of the body pale. The longer you hang a chicken, the more intense the flavour, so kill and pluck it on one day, hang it overnight, and then dress the bird the next evening.

DRESSING BIRDS

Dressing a bird is the final part of the preparation process and involves removing all of the parts of the chicken that you don't want to cook, such as the wing tips, feet, head and neck and innards.

The wing tips are removed because the feathers here are very difficult to pluck, making it simpler just to chop off the wing tips themselves. Look closely at the wings, and you will see a patch of white gristle about 2.5 cm (1 in) from each tip; chop off the wing tips at this point.

The next thing to do is to remove the feet and tendons. To do this, first cut the skin just below the knee, around the front and both sides, but not at the back. Then position the leg over the edge of a work surface and strike it sharply to break the bone. Next, pull the leg really hard to remove the tendon from the back of the leg. You may need to twist the tendon round the broken bone to draw it out gradually, but be careful because the tendon

will suddenly break. Once you have removed the tendon, cut away the remaining piece of shinbone, taking it back to the knuckle of the knee.

Next to come off are the head and neck, and be warned that this is the messiest part of the dressing process because the bird's blood will have collected within the neck while it was hanging upside down. Cut off the head at the point where the neck was broken, then peel back the skin as far as possible and force the neck backwards, over the body: this breaks the neck again at the shoulder point, and you can now cut into the flesh around the neck and remove it. Split the neck's skin down to the breastbone and remove the crop.

Now you're ready to tackle the far end of the bird, and to cut, very carefully, around the anus. When doing this, be careful not to cut too deeply into the flesh and sever the intestines. First, pinch the flesh at the base of the breastbone and cut across the body halfway between that point and the anus. Then, from each end of the incision, cut down to either side of the anus. Now cut across the base of the parson's nose; this final cut should release the anus so that the innards can be re-

moved, and should create a hole big enough for you to be able to insert your hand into the body cavity. Pull away the severed anus and surrounding skin, but don't pull too hard, otherwise you'll tear the intestines and will spill their contents into the carcass' cavity.

Next, reach inside the carcass, run your fingers all the way around the cavity and release anything that is attached to its inner walls by firmly gripping the innards and pulling gently, but steadily. With a bit of luck – and practice – most of the innards will come out in one piece. The liver and the stomach wall (which can be split lengthwise until you reach the lining, which can be removed with the stomach's contents) can be retained for making chicken stock or gravy, as can the neck. If the bird is a cockerel, then you may be quite surprised by the size of his testicles (in the tradition of many Far Eastern cuisines, these are considered quite a delicacy). If the bird is a hen, you'll find several partly developed eggs alongside the innards. Note that the innards must be handled very carefully and removed quite gently. Tucked away within the mass you'll find the chicken's gall bladder, and if this bursts and spills its contents of bile

on to the flesh, the meat will be spoiled, and the bird will have been wasted. So the gall bladder, which is attached to the liver, needs to be trimmed off very carefully, and remember that it's better to lose a bit of liver than to cut into the gall bladder.

The chicken's remaining internal parts are the lungs, bright-red organs attached to the ribs, which you can either leave in place or remove by digging your finger behind them and pulling them away from the bone.

Now wash out the inside of the bird with lots of clean, running water (you should do this with any bird, even one bought from a supermarket). Dry the bird with paper towels before singeing off any remaining feathers and stubble using a burning spill. Then wash and dry the bird again.

The final stage before seasoning or stuffing the chicken and placing it in the oven is securing the legs. Do this by either making two cuts in the skin on the bird's sides and tucking the legs through them or tying the knuckles to the parson's nose.

Apart from its tender and tasty flesh, there is one thing that may surprise you when you eat your first home-reared chicken: the toughness of the skin. A shop-bought bird is likely to have been only about five weeks old when it died, and will therefore have soft, babyish, tender skin. Your bird, by contrast, will probably have been about six months old when you despatched it, and will no doubt have led a pretty full and active life running around and enjoying the air in your garden. You can, if you prefer, remove the roasted skin before carving the flesh. Or, if you are a keen cook, you could skin and bone the bird entirely before cooking it according to your preferred recipe. Bon appetit!

CHAPTER NINE

Pests and parasites, diseases and other health problems

Chickens are pretty hardy creatures, and keeping them can, for the most part, be trouble-free. Nevertheless, there are pest and parasites, diseases and ailments of which you need to be aware, as well as of how they should be treated. The information that follows is not designed to replace the professional advice of veterinarians, but is instead intended to give you an idea of what might be wrong with a chicken so that you don't panic.

Remember that although many of the ailments suffered by chickens can be remedied with the right medication, as with all aspects of health maintenance, prevention is better than cure, and there are a number of ways in which you can prevent your birds from becoming seriously ill, as outlined below.

Good hygiene, housing and diet

Good hygiene, housing and diet are essential to chickens' health, productivity and welfare. So always ensure that:

- you maintain a scrupulous daily cleaning routine;
- your chickens are kept in henhouses and runs that are clean (and make sure that they are cleaned before it becomes necessary to do so);
- your chickens are kept in well-ventilated henhouses: there should be no drafts to chill the birds, but the atmosphere should never be stuffy either;
- your chickens are housed in coops and runs where there is sufficient space for each bird because overcrowding causes stress and can lead to sickness;
- you routinely scrub feeders and drinkers clean; buy a bucket and scrubbing brushes and label them 'For chicken use only' to prevent any cross-contamination. If sick or ailing birds need to be quarantined in separate accommodation, make sure that their feeders and drinkers are cleaned separately – with different buckets and brushes – to ensure that illness is not passed from them to the healthy birds (note that birds in quarantine should also have their droppings tested by a vet);
- your birds are fed a well-balanced diet;
- your birds' feed is the right mix and size for their age and needs;
- any perishable food that has not been eaten is removed from the henhouse every day;
- food is stored in well-sealed containers in a cool, dry place where it cannot be contaminated; make sure that it is fresh, not past its sell-by date, mouldy or damp before feeding it to your chickens;
- birds are wormed and vaccinated against incurable diseases.

Remember this motto: 'Neglect and Disease make fine bedfellows, and Death is the lodger who moves in with them'.

Bio-security

As a result of the concerns raised by avian influenza (see pages 216 to 217), the use of the term 'bio-security' has become more common, and while the small-scale chicken-keeper needs to be as vigilant as the commercial poultry producer, much of what is described as 'bio-security' actually comprises common-sense hygiene measures. The most important aspects of this are the removal of droppings from the run and feeding chickens in an area that is not accessible to wild birds. These are the two main ways in which bird-to-bird infection occurs, but for added bio-security, placing a footbath filled with disinfectant at the entrance to your poultry 'yard' in which to dip your shoes on entry and exit will mean that you are complying with the recommendations made by government scientists and veterinarians. It's a simple, but highly effective, means of ensuring that you do not introduce infection or disease to your birds, so get into the habit of using a foot-bath right from the start of your chicken-keeping adventure.

Warning signs

The most effective way of checking the health of your birds is to spend a little time just watching them and their behaviour each day. The more familiar you become with your birds, their habits and their behaviour, the more adept you will become at spotting and dealing with any problems that may occur.

Chickens are very sociable creatures and like to be part of the flock, so the first sign that there is something wrong with a bird is if it has retreated to a corner where it is sitting and moping. Remember that when they are awake, chickens should always be scratching around in the ground, taking dust-baths or feeding, and that the combs of most breeds should be red and waxy, while their eyes should be bright. Drooping wings, ruffled feathers, sudden gain or loss of appetite and loose, wet droppings stuck to the feathers around the vent are an indication that a bird needs treatment.

If a bird is tame enough to be picked up, examine it thoroughly for signs of mites, fleas and lice underneath its wings and where there are downy feathers. At the same time, take the opportunity to feel the chicken's breast on either side of its keel (breastbone) for any signs of weight loss.

A few symptoms of diseases and parasites that you can check for follow:

- itchiness;
- bare patches;
- weight loss;
- diarrhoea;
- symptoms of paralysis;

- swollen legs with scales that are standing up;
- a laying hen that has stopped laying eggs (note, however, that as the birds enter their annual moult, they will also stop laying);
- a bird that is sitting hunched up, with ruffled feathers.

What to do if a bird looks ill

If a chicken appears to be ill, or you suspect that it might be, immediately remove it from the flock and keep it separate from the other birds. Chickens are no respecters of another bird's ill-health, and will, given the opportunity, begin to peck, attack and injure it. Place the ailing bird somewhere quiet, where it can rest, and make sure that it is kept warm: a heat lamp or heating pad is often the only treatment that a bird requires in order to regain its strength and vitality. And in many instances, a bird that looks a little peaky or off-colour will have revived within 24 hours.

Getting help

If you are a newcomer to chicken-keeping, a health scare can be upsetting. The most important thing is to stay calm and to contact an experienced chicken-breeder, local poultry club or vet (preferably one with knowledge of chickens) as soon as possible. Any of these should be able to offer support, advice, knowledge and expertise, helping you to regain your confidence and take action if necessary.

Pests and parasites

Keep an eye open for the following pests and parasites to which chickens are vulnerable.

LICE

Lice are small, chewing insects that feed on the scales of feathers, dry skin, skin debris and scabs. The common fowl louse (*Menopon gallinae*) is fast-moving, light-brown in colour and flattish in shape, and an infestation of these pests is extremely irritating for birds.

Chickens deal with lice to a large extent by dust-bathing: rolling around in the dust chokes the lice and makes them fall off the bird's body. Nevertheless, there will always be lice that manage to survive. Fortunately, there are a number of highly effective proprietary sprays and powders available with which to treat lice infestations, but prevention is better than cure, and a weekly examination of your chickens should alert you to any outbreak. Your chickens should be free of lice when you buy and collect them, but it only takes one or two unhatched eggs that have been laid in the birds' feathers for them to breed. A weekly dusting of the nesting boxes will help to stop hens from being infested by lice, but note that cock birds will need to be treated individually. Chickens that have been hen-pecked should be routinely checked for lice.

A good time to inspect your chickens for lice is when they have settled on their perches at night: they are easier to pick up when they are asleep! Lice's main areas of activity are around a chicken's vent and on the thighs and neck, but you should also check its crest for signs of infestation. And if you do find any lice, sprinkle or spray a recommended treatment under the feathers (do this outside on a night when it's not too windy so that the powder or spray won't be blown away). A bad infestation of lice will manifest itself as clusters of little grey-coloured eggs – or nits – on the feathers around a chicken's vent. These eggs are nearly impossible to shift, although you could try trimming off any longer tail feathers that have eggs attached to them and then burning them. Repeated applications of the anti-louse powder or spray (remember to follow the manufacturer's instructions) will be necessary to kill the lice as they hatch on other parts of the body.

FLEAS

Most people know that cats and dogs get fleas, but fewer are aware that chickens can also play host to these parasites. Chicken fleas (*Echidnophaga gallinacea*) are clearly visible to the naked eye: they have six legs and hop when discovered. Signs of flea infestation may include apparently itchy skin; weight loss; bare patches amid the feathers; and a pale, anaemic-looking comb and wattles (due to blood loss caused by feasting fleas).

Because fleas thrive in warm and humid conditions, infestations are more likely to break out during the summer, so inspect your chickens regularly (and at least weekly) at this time of year. Infested birds need to be treated with a proprietary flea powder or spray, and because most of the flea population is to be found in their accommodation rather than on the chickens themselves, note that all of their houses' internal surfaces also need to be treated in order to kill the fleas' eggs, larvae and pupae.

MITES

There are several species of mites that infest chickens, three of which can be particularly troublesome: scaly leg mite, northern fowl mite and the red mite.

Scaly leg mite

Scaly leg mite (*Cnemiodocoptes mutans*) causes disfigurement to a chicken's legs whereby they become swollen, itchy and look rather horn-like, with the scales starting to stand up and grey crusts beginning to form between them (these crusts are, in fact, the excrement produced by the mite). In severe cases, the chicken's leg flesh may become inflamed and start bleeding, and the bird may eventually have great difficulty walking.

Because the scaly leg mite is a parasite that is not visible to the naked eye, the first signs of any problem with the scales on a chicken's legs will need immediate attention. Liberally apply petroleum jelly to the bird's legs, leave it to be absorbed for two or three days and then carefully, and gently, use a soft brush and lukewarm water to clean off any scabs and crusts (but don't attempt to remove any dry scales as this will cause bleeding). Next, apply a proprietary anti-scabies medication to the bird's legs (this is available from veterinary surgeries). To prevent reoccurrence, clean and disinfect the henhouse thoroughly or treat it with a proprietary anti-parasite solution. Note that because the scaly leg mite thrives in damp, humid conditions, it is vital that henhouses are properly ventilated. Chickens are often infected with scaly leg mites at an early age, and because the mites are transmitted from chicken to chicken – not via people or other animals – hens should be given a preventative treatment before their eggs hatch.

Northern fowl mite

Most domestic poultry (and probably all wild birds) are hosts to *Ornythonyssus sylviarum*, or the northern fowl mite. While chickens' feathers can be damaged by too small a pop-hole or sharp edges inside their houses or runs, these mites can also cause damage and ill-health. Most often, it is the tail and wings that are affected, although you also need to check birds thoroughly all over, especially around the vent area. (The crests and beards of breeds with these features will also need to be constantly inspected.) Telltale signs of their presence are feathers that look as though they've been chewed or gnawed at, with blackened damp patches, because the mites settle in these places and hide in the feather follicles. If your chickens have lice, you may be heartened to know that they probably won't be affected by northern fowl mites, too, because it seems that these two parasites dislike each other's presence and won't – or can't – share the same host.

Northern fowl mites are grey or black in colour and are often visible as a mass of pin-head-sized moving bodies. Because these mites are bloodsuckers, they can cause great debilitation in chickens, and can also transmit other diseases. Powders and sprays are available with which to treat chickens with infestations of these mites. When using them, make sure that the treatment is dabbed onto the birds' ears – but avoid their eyes – as this mite sometimes hides in the ear canals, so that just when you think that you've got rid of the lot, another batch emerges. A single treatment is rarely sufficient, so ensure that you apply follow-up treatments, and don't forget to clean out and disinfect the henhouse, and to dust or spray the nesting boxes.

Red mite

In spite of its name, the red mite (*Dermanyssus gallinae*) is greyish-white in colour, and only becomes red after feeding on a chicken's blood (it feeds at night, when the bird is asleep). The red mite is related to spiders, and although its eight legs are quite visible to the naked eye, because of its nocturnal habits, the only way to spot it is with a torch at night, when the chickens are roosting.

Red-mite infestation must be taken very seriously because not only can these parasites seriously affect the health of your chickens, they can also be the carriers of diseases like Newcastle disease, fowl pox and avian diphtheria (see pages 218 to 219). And the irritation that red mites inflict on chickens is severe, sometimes causing them to pluck out their own feathers in an attempt to gain relief, and making a broody hen so uncomfortable that they can drive her from sitting on her clutch of eggs.

To prevent your chickens from being infected, it's vital that the interior surfaces of their henhouse are as smooth and even as possible because the mites live in joints, nooks and crannies (around the door jambs, under window ledges and in corners, for instance). You will also find them on the under side of perches, which is why they – and the notches, slots or holders into which the perches fit – must be routinely removed, cleaned and disinfected. Expert poultry-keepers can detect red-mite infestations by the smell in the henhouse and the presence of a grey-coloured dust in the coop, this dust being, in fact, the mites' cast-off skins. It really can't be stressed enough that the cause of red-mite infestation lies within the henhouse. So clean every inch of it (if you can, use a pressure-washer) and then wash it with a solution of water and strong disinfectant. Let the henhouse dry thoroughly before allowing the chickens back inside. Also first sprinkle plenty of wood-shavings over the floor to absorb the moisture, and then replace them with fresh, dry shavings before allowing the birds in again.

If a red-mite infestation is confirmed, then you will also need to treat the chickens, as well as their housing, with a proprietary treatment. Note that you'll need to repeat this treatment as red mites are pretty tough creatures and can survive for quite long periods without feeding.

WORMS

Chickens can contract various types of worms. Sometimes, the only indication of their presence is that a chicken starts to lose weight or develops diarrhoea; infected birds may also have an increased appetite, while at the same time producing fewer eggs. Their combs will usually also look pink, rather than red, because these worms are bloodsuckers, and birds who are suffering from heavy infestations will often pass bundles of dead worms with their droppings.

The two main types of worms that affect chickens are tapeworms and roundworms. Tapeworms have flat, segmented bodies; roundworms have round, smooth bodies. Both are generally passed from bird to bird via their droppings (which is why it is so important to clean the henhouse regularly), fertilised worms being excreted and picked up by other birds. The rear segments of tapeworms periodically break off and are excreted as well, as are also tapeworm eggs, which are then eaten by snails, beetles and woodlice, which are in turn eaten by chickens (especially those that roam free); they can also be carried around on the shoes of keepers, which is another bio-security reason why a disinfectant footbath is recommended (see page 203). Medications and preventative treatments are available with which to treat tapeworm and roundworm infestation, which should be administered twice a year, during the spring and autumn. The medication may be given to chickens by mixing it into moistened mash; alternatively, water-soluble treatments can be added to drinkers.

In addition to tapeworms and roundworms, two further types of worms may appear in the oesophagus, crop and mouth of a chicken: *Capillaria contorta* and *C. annulata*, tiny, thread-like worms that are too small to be seen with the naked eye. The larvae of these worms develop inside the common garden earthworm, which chickens are particularly partial to as a tasty treat. Once inside a bird, the larvae develop into worms that attach their heads to the lining of the bird's mouth, crop and sometimes also the oesophagus, causing a thick layer of dead and dying cells that reduces that part of the digestive system's normal contractions. With their digestion thus impaired, chickens will start to lose weight. Preventative treatment with proprietary products is therefore advised twice yearly, during the spring and summer.

Diseases

Chickens are especially vulnerable to the following diseases.

MYCOPLASMA

Most chickens in the UK carry mycoplasma, but this disease lies dormant inside them. That said, if a bird becomes ill with another ailment, is kept in poor or overcrowded conditions or is severely stressed, an outbreak of 'myco' may be triggered. Mycoplasma is a very serious respiratory disease that can strike chickens in a number of forms, most commonly as *Mycoplasma gallisepticum*. In this instance, the disease is spread through egg or aerosol transmission (that is, by tiny droplets of infected moisture spread by chickens' sneezes and coughs) and through direct contact with already infected birds.

Mycoplasma causes chronic respiratory problems and air-sac syndrome: affected birds sneeze, cough and produce a mucus discharge from their nostrils; their eyes become runny; and, in the worst cases, their air sacs fill with matter. The birds also become droopy and lethargic, have a reduced appetite and consequently lose weight rapidly; cockerels stop crowing because their throats are sore. Antibiotics are the only treatment for this disease (although there is evidence to suggest a growing resistance to them), and because the infection spreads very rapidly, if you suspect mycoplasma in a bird, you must immediately consult your vet so that treatment can be given at once. The next thing that you must do is to try to identify the root cause of the outbreak – which may often be stress, overcrowding and or housing – and then remedy it.

MAREK'S DISEASE

Marek's disease affects primarily commercial flocks, and some breeds of chickens, such as Silkies and Sebrights, are more at risk from it than others. Most adult birds will have been vaccinated against Marek's disease as day-old chicks, but, as with all medicines, there is some evidence of reduced immunity to it due to widespread vaccination among commercial flocks.

The disease is spread through dust particles, including dust made by feather follicles shed from newly grown feathers. The problem normally occurs in young birds between 12 and 16 weeks of age, and affects mainly hens. As they approach the point of lay, hens' hormone levels change, and the signs of Marek's disease become evident: their wings and legs appear paralysed, and they look really sick. Once they have reached this stage of the disease, there is no cure for it, which means that they must be culled as humanely as possible.

AVIAN INFLUENZA

Until recently, few people outside the chicken world had heard of avian influenza, or 'bird flu', as the media has called it. There are many strains of this virus, but it's the H5N1 one that has caused the most concern, prompting the destruction of millions of birds across Europe and South East Asia in an attempt to control its spread. Not only fatal to chickens, but also to humans, the virus is highly contagious, and is caught through contact with faeces or air expelled by infected birds. It is spread by all birds (not just chickens), and migratory waterfowl are particularly effective carriers. The visible signs of infection are essentially limited to the 'bluing' of a bird's comb and wattles, and sudden death.
The only way of preventing avian influenza in chickens is to increase bio-security measures to avoid healthy birds having any contact with infected birds, including wild birds. This means using enclosed

runs and bird-proof netting (or, better still, runs with solid roofs). The deadly consequences of this disease mean that government authorities take suspected outbreaks very seriously, with exclusion zones being set up around the centre of any outbreak and all birds within them being culled.

COCCIDIOSIS

Coccidiosis is a potentially fatal disease that affects young chickens aged between three and six weeks old. Chicks receive no immunity from the mother hen, and only gradually acquire resistance to the disease after low-level exposure to it, becoming fully immune at about seven weeks of age. In order to minimise the risk of infection, for the first 16 weeks of their lives, chicks should be fed a proprietary chick crumb containing an anticoccidiosis agent (note that bags of chick-crumb feed should be marked with the letters 'ACS').

The typical symptoms of coccidiosis include depression, a hunched-up sitting position, ruffled feathers, a white soiling around the vent area, paleness and often bloody diarrhoea. The disease usually occurs in hot weather, but damp, lack of ventilation and poor hygiene can also stimulate an outbreak. If you suspect that a chicken has coccidiosis, then you must have its droppings analysed by a vet, who, if its presence is confirmed, will then provide preparations with which to treat the disease. Coccidiosis is spread through birds' droppings, so these must be removed from the henhouse and lime should then be scattered over the floor, after which a solution of ammonia should be applied in order to trap the protozoa that cause the disease within a solid slab of plaster-like substance that can be safely removed and disposed of. It probably also goes without saying that the coop, run and all other items used by your chickens must always be kept scrupulously clean. In addition, a disinfectant footbath (or disposable paper or plastic shoe slip covers) for your use when entering and leaving the birds' enclosure will go a long way in minimising any outbreak.

FOWL POX AND AVIAN DIPHTHERIA

Caused by various viruses, fowl pox (or avian cholera) is identifiable by grey-black ulcers or lumps on the heads of chickens, but only on the skin. If these occur in the mouth, then the disease is called avian diphtheria, but it is essentially the same infection, which is usually caused by insect bites, particularly those of mosquitoes (which can be a problem in certain regions, climates and seasons). A vaccination is available against fowl pox and avian diphtheria, but in the event of an outbreak, the ulcers are often treated with a tincture of iodine.

NEWCASTLE DISEASE (NCD)

Newcastle Disease (NCD), or avian pneumoencephalitis, is a fatal viral disease whose presence is indicated by a combination of green droppings and the total paralysis of infected birds, with accompanying symptoms including ruffled feathers, sitting in a hunched-up position and breathing difficulties. While there is no cure for NCD, there is a vaccination against it (which is compulsory before entering chickens at shows in most countries), and members of poultry-breeders' clubs are able to join collective vaccination programmes that ensure that birds are protected for up to three months.

Chickens are prone to certain other health problems, so look out for the following.

Other health problems

DIARRHOEA

A healthy chicken's normal droppings are a greenish-brown colour, with a little white mixed in, while their texture is rather dry. Diarrhoea is therefore a sign that something is wrong. It may just be that you have shocked the birds by changing their usual feed, and if the diarrhoea is only mild, try giving the chickens some ground charcoal to eat. If the diarrhoea is very watery or contains signs of blood, however, and your chickens are losing weight and are listless, they may have coccidiosis (see above, pages 217 to 218). Remember, too, that infestations by worms can also cause diarrhoea (see above, pages 213 to 214).

BUMBLEFOOT

Bumblefoot – when chickens have swollen feet – is an avoidable complaint. This painful condition is caused by birds jumping unnecessarily, and is often the consequence of their perches being too high for them to reach or descend from, so that they land on a hard floor. So make sure that their perches and any 'mangers' dispensing green stuff are located at the right height for your chickens to be able to access them safely and comfortably.

FROZEN HEAD FURNISHINGS

During a hard frost, chickens' featherless parts, such as their combs and wattles, can become frozen. The problem is more acute in breeds with large combs (breeds with smaller, rose combs are less likely to suffer). It is caused when atmospheric moisture settles on the combs and wattles while the birds are roosting in an insulated space at night, so that when they go out on a frosty morning, the moisture freezes. The affected, frozen tissue then becomes discoloured as sections (or all) of the combs and wattles die; in cocks, this can cause infertility the following spring. The best way to avoid frozen head furnishings is to make sure that your chickens' housing is well ventilated (although not draughty), with enough air circulating to prevent condensation from building up inside. In cold weather, you could also smear your birds' combs and wattles with some acid-free petroleum jelly to prevent them from becoming chapped.

CROP AND GIZZARD IMPACTION

At the base of a chicken's neck is the crop, which is easy to see when it is full as it bulges, and you can feel it, too. Food is held within the crop until it is soft enough to be passed on to the next stage of digestion. Because chickens can't chew, long, fibrous foods – long blades of grass and fibrous stalks, for instance – can become tangled in a ball in the crop, forming a plug that can't pass on to the oesophagus. When the chicken next eats something, the blockage in the crop causes the neck to become distended and swollen, and it feels very hard to the touch. This is crop impaction, and the owner then has to remove the blockage. This is done by running some warm water down the chicken's throat – remembering to give it time to breathe – massaging the crop and then tipping the bird upside down and continuing to massage the crop until the chicken expels its contents through its mouth. This action is a bit scary, and rather tricky, for a novice chicken-keeper to carry out, so it's best to contact a more experienced person or vet for help in teaching you the correct technique. Note that the problem can be avoided if your birds eat only short grass, so don't feed them clippings and keep them away from meadows and other areas where there are tough, fibrous grasses.

If the crop keeps refilling, even when the bird is kept on short grass or in a run, the problem may be gizzard impaction. In this case, grass and other matter has passed through the crop, but has formed a long rope that is blocking the top of the intestines. This is a much more serious condition, and you will need a vet's help to remedy it. Yet this, too, can often be avoided by giving your birds grit (see pages 127 to 128). Although gizzard impaction especially affects young birds that have been put out on their first patch of grass because their gizzards haven't yet developed sufficiently to cope with it, it can also occur in other birds that aren't swallowing enough dietary grit. Remember that grit is a vital component in chicken feed, and that it should always be available to your birds.

index

Bibliography

Basson, F, *Mini Encyclopedia: Chicken Breeds and Care*, Interpret Publishing, 2009.

Eastoe, J, *Henkeeping*, Anova Books, 2007.

Graham, C, *Choosing and Keeping Chickens*, Hamlyn (in association with *Practical Poultry* magazine), 2006.

Hatcher, M, *Hen Keeping: Self-sufficiency*, New Holland, 2009.

Hobson, J, and Lewis, C, *Keeping Chickens: The Essential Guide to Enjoying and Getting the Best from Chickens*, David & Charles, 2009.

Luttman, R and G, *Chickens in Your Backyard*, Rodale Press, 1976.

Megyesi, J, *The Joy of Keeping Chickens*, Skyhorse Publishing, 2009.

Raymond, F, *The Big Book of Garden Hens*, Kitchen Garden Books, 2001.

Shirt, V, *The Right Way to Keep Chickens*, Right Way Books, 2008.

Verhoeff, E, and Rijs, A, *The Complete Encylopedia of Chickens*, Rebo Publishing, 2009.

Woolnoough, M, *Raising Chickens for Eggs and Meat*, Good Life Press, 2009.

Magazines and websites

Poultry magazine, issued with *Country Smallholding* magazine

Practical Poultry magazine (www.practicalpolutry.co.uk)

www.poultryclub.org (Poultry Club)

www.poultrykeeper.com

www.bhwt.org.uk (Battery Hen Welfare Trust)

www.littlehenrescue.co.uk (battery-hen rescue and rehoming organisation)

www.free-at-last.org.uk (battery-hen rescue and rehoming)

www.feathersite.com

www.poultrypages.com

www.hsa.org.uk (Humane Slaughter Association)

www.rbst.org.uk (Rare Breeds Survival Trust)

Credits and acknowledgments

Thanks to Diana, Gloria, Mark and Rob, and to all the chicken enthusiasts who gave their time and advice so freely.